Praise

"Danielle is a force field of energy, wonder, humor, and love."

V (formerly Eve Ensler)

author of The Vagina Monologues *and* In the Body of the World

"When I think of Danielle LaPorte, what comes to heart and mind is a woman who practices what she teaches. She radiates authenticity, compassion, deep caring, intelligence, and a true desire for others to transform their lives into their greater yet-to-be. She's the Real Deal!"

Rev. Michael Bernard Beckwith

founder of Agape International Spiritual Center, author of Life Visioning

"Danielle LaPorte is a bright light in the modern priestesshood. She keeps it spiritual, she keeps it real, she keeps it good."

Marianne Williamson

New York Times *bestselling author of* A Return to Love

"Our souls are yearning for Danielle's liberating message—that discernment is crucial to our true spiritual freedom. She's as compassionate as she is fiery, and every contemporary seeker will see themselves in her . . ."

Shefali Tsabary, PhD

New York Times *bestselling author of* The Awakened Family

"Danielle is . . . a woman who's made a tremendous impact on my life with her brave and badass approach to living a heart centered life."

LeAnn Rimes Cibrian

singer/songwriter, host of the Wholly Human *podcast*

"Danielle is the living embodiment of heart centered leadership. Her approach to her life and her offerings ooze love and generosity and show us how we can live and give full out."

John Wineland

founder of The New Men's Work Project, author of From the Core

"Danielle is a real-deal, no-BS teacher with an incredible depth of wisdom. **She's built a timeless library of content. Her content is unique and highly relevant, and her style of delivery makes it so lovely to consume.** Danielle leads with both her heart and super intelligent mind. Her words are medicine; her body of work is life-changing."

Christine Hassler

master life coach, author of Expectation Hangover

"Danielle LaPorte never disappoints as this generation's *go-to* truth-teller and visionary, always leading by being ahead of the curve. She intuits what is needed and provides it at the exact right moment."

Terri Cole

psychotherapist, author of Boundary Boss

"Danielle's voice is medicine for self-help fatigue and ambition overdrive. Her deep clarity and realness are a healing combination—and it's right on time for our culture."

Mark Hyman, MD

ten-time New York Times *bestselling author*

"A beacon of compassion, Danielle is an extraordinary human. A woman devoted to helping people transcend their limitations, and access their potential, and truly self-actualize. Honest, accessible, and authentic to the core."

Rich Roll

host of The Rich Roll Podcast*, vegan activist, athlete*

"Danielle lights the way in reconnecting people to their true voice and authentic self. Her words hold the power to validate, heal, and free the hearts and souls of humankind."

Anthony William

#1 New York Times *bestselling author of the Medical Medium series*

HOW TO BE LOVING

while your heart is breaking open
and our world is waking up

A HEART CENTERED
APPROACH TO LIVING

Also available as an audiobook + e-book,
with a companion journal and deck

sounds true
BOULDER, COLORADO

Sounds True
Boulder, CO 80306

Published 2022

Cover design by Danielle LaPorte, Lisa Kerans, Cheryl Sorg
Book design by Connie Poole
Author photo by Anastasia Chomlack
Cover art by Cheryl Sorg | CherylSorg.com

Printed in the United States of America

BK06147

Library of Congress Cataloging-in-Publication Data
Names: LaPorte, Danielle, 1969- author.
Title: How to be loving : as your heart is breaking open and our world is
    waking up / Danielle LaPorte.
Description: Boulder, CO : Sounds True, [2022]
Identifiers: LCCN 2021061726 (print) | LCCN 2021061727 (ebook) | ISBN
    9781683647621 (hardback) | ISBN 9781683647638 (ebook)
Subjects: LCSH: Love. | Fear. | Compassion. | Ego (Psychology)
Classification: LCC BF575.L8 L2677 2022 (print) | LCC BF575.L8 (ebook) |
    DDC 152.4/1--dc23/eng/20220401
LC record available at https://lccn.loc.gov/2021061726
LC ebook record available at https://lccn.loc.gov/2021061727

10 9 8 7 6 5 4 3 2 1

" . . . everything exposed by the light becomes visible—
and everything that is illuminated becomes a light."

–Ephesians 5:13

CONTENTS

INTRODUCTION

ON MY MOST RECENT YEAR-IN-REVIEW exercise, I seriously considered walking away from my creative life (which I tend to reconsider every few years). I had this romantic notion of meditating all morning in my apartment, growing potatoes on my deck for neighbors, wearing white peasant blouses, and never checking my Instagram *ever again*.

But instead, I came to my senses and wrote this book.

Because my heart is breaking (open) from the state of this world. I think we're longing for Love and Truth—and for each other.

My life used to be guided by the question "How do I want to feel?" I built my career on that with *The Desire Map* book. But I began to notice that even if I wasn't experiencing my core desired feelings, I was still in touch with a greater purpose. Temporary unhappiness didn't hold me back from helping out a friend or feeling useful or close to the Divine.

A new question emerged: "What do I want to embody?" And the answer was clear: Love. Love, no matter what.

●

Shifting from an emotion-driven life to a more heart centered life is a developmental process. The path to being more Loving is through a Loving process itself. It's gentle and compassionate. It's about creating a friendship with reality.

Being Loving doesn't mean feeling *more*. It means feeling everything *with more Love*.

This is a book about Acceptance and Unity Consciousness. It's not a map, it's an urgent Love letter to the Light in every one of us. I hope it helps us remember who we are, together.

With Love,

Danielle
xo

ALL
HEART

Chapter 1

JOURNEY TO THE CENTER OF YOUR HEART

Spirituality is the practice of thinking with Love.

Your heart is open.

All of the time, actually. You can't ever close your heart—no matter what. We only think that we open or close our hearts. Our mind manufactures thoughts that veil our Loving awareness, like clouds floating through the sky. Some happiness billows by. There goes a wisp of concern. A rain cloud of worry. Starry ideas. The clouds of emotions, thoughts, and pure inspiration are naturally coming and going, and all the while there's the sky itself accommodating absolutely everything in its vastness and multitasking with galaxies. The sky is being, allowing, and expanding. The sky doesn't ever constrict. It can only be the sky discovering more of its sky-ness.

The same is true for your heart, your true Loving nature. It's always present, always opening to more of your trueness. No amount of any kind of thinking can alter your true Loving nature. Just as no weather pattern can swallow the sky, there's no emotional pattern that can affect your divinity. There are just thought formations passing through limitless, luminous space—your heart.

We don't "close our hearts" to one another, ourselves, or the things that happen. We just shut down our minds, like closing blackout curtains on the sun. **Spirituality is really just the practice of open-mindedness, of intentionally not putting up blocks to life.** We open up our minds and we keep finding this incredible heart energy always pulsating for us—eternally patient, endlessly vibrant.

Enlightenment is when the mind fans out so wide that it dissolves into unbounded Loving awareness. We go from thinking to pure being. In the sky of the heart, there aren't walls of identity to get in the way of Unity. The heart doesn't use personality hang-ups or political opinions to spar about the so-called truth.

The heart's Wisdom blows personality constructs to stardust, and it lays the True Reality bare.

In the heart center, everything is seen for what it is, and it's all welcomed. All of it. THAT'S true Love. That's Divine Love.

When we're curious about and committed to Loving, we think very differently. Rather than thoughts that act as Love blockades, more *unifying* thoughts rise up from our intention to Love. We don't have to go looking for "higher" thoughts outside of ourselves. We just have to be still often enough to realize that we're part of something infinitely creative and inclusive. This happens in increments.

●

Open-mindedness—spirituality—is the practice of thinking with Love. And we can effectively train ourselves to keep returning to Love via our thoughts. First, we refer to our heart's mind for the best way to proceed. Then we recruit the mental mind to support the heart. This is what it means to have our priorities straight. First, let the Love flow, then direct that Love with your intelligence. This is divine order.

When Love is in our mind, we form fewer conclusions about who's "worthy" or "unworthy," what's right versus wrong, or whether it's too late or right on time. Love sees the perfection in the person and the moment and proceeds from that expanded awareness. It's like zooming out to notice both the sun's rays and the chemtrails and choosing to comment on how amazing the sky is. When you open your mind to see what's really going on—with a person, in any situation, the beautiful parts become more evident.

Insight begins with the desire to truly know what's truly going on. It's as simple as pausing in the middle of an emotional bind with someone and thinking, *I wonder what* they're *experiencing now?* That's an act of Love.

Reflecting

In order to see the whole picture and everything in it, we have to slow down. We have to be still to actually reflect on what's happening—and what might be true or false about what's happening. Reflection is a heart practice. Stillness and contemplation are how we tap the vitality of the heart—which is limitless.

When we live more reflectively, we operate less reactively. With every meditation or earnest question . . . with each honest prayer, given blessing, or intimate conversation that we have—with ourselves or each other—the heart is giving us confirmation about how massively beautiful life really is. The heart will always choose to focus on what's working.

But many of us aren't raised to live very reflective lives. And our productivity-obsessed culture won't have any of it. Instead of **reflection, receptivity, and responsiveness**, we tie ourselves to a looping track of reactiveness. And then we mostly sleepwalk through the days, inevitably get hammered by some kind of painful occurrence, and then we wake up to glimpse a higher purpose. And if we don't dedicate our lives to that higher purpose—**to Love**—then we'll probably doze off until the next bout of hard-to-bear discomfort or loss arrives. We think we're really smart with our strategies for status and self-preservation, but running from Love while looking out for #1 is a high form of foolishness. Because Unconditional Love is what we want the most.

> **Regardless of our status and no matter how many degrees, followers, or pretty things we own, no matter how much we've accomplished or overcome in the material world, what we yearn for is to rest in Love. We want to relax into the Great Heart—the heart that holds us all—and to feel Creation carrying us.** It's the freedom of union. It's the liberation of belonging to each other.

There are ways to get free—free of the madness of the world we've made— and to be at ease. There are metaphysical, superconscious, ancient, and scientifically proven ways: mindful breathing, visualization and meditation, acts of kindness, community building, Forgiving each other, getting good sleep, healthy eating, joyful movement . . . Loving who we Love, full on and full out, and then including ourselves and all beings in that Love.

A heart centered life is a reflective life. And a reflective life becomes energized with the Light of Love and higher virtues.

When you get still and take the time to consider how beautiful life truly is, you'll have more Compassion and Acceptance for the ugliness and chaos. Your stillness will increase your capacity for holding the dichotomies and paradoxes of your life. And then it will become more apparent that we are all participating in an ongoing miracle. Looking within is how we awaken to the True Reality—because it has never been outside of us.

It's only a Loving gaze that can see the Truth.

It takes some (spiritual) practice. But if you become still more often and you look inward, you will see that your heart is as open as the sky.

"Meditate on the Self as being
Vast as the sky.
A body of energy
Extending forever in all directions—
Above, below, all around.

In the embrace of the infinite space,
Awaken to your true form,
Divine creative energy
Revealing Herself as you."

  –*The Radiance Sutras,*
    as translated by Lorin Roche

Love it all.
Love it all.
Love it all.
Love it all.
Love it all.
Love it all.
Love it all.
Love it all.
Love it all.

Chapter 2

HEALING IS NONLINEAR

The more you give and receive Love, the more Truth (and nontruth) you'll be able to recognize in all areas of life.

BRING TO MIND A SIGNIFICANT PAIN POINT in your life, something that you've already done a lot of healing work on. Maybe you did the therapy and came to some resolution. You've had a dozen insights, and you're feeling liberated from the original cause of sorrow. Or you've walked miles and miles, letting all the layers go. Did the workshop *and* the cleanse. Went to the desert, burned it, *and* buried it. You're *good*.

The release was real. The Forgiveness was authentic. The progress was legit. How do you know? Because you experience more peacefulness than you did before. You're a better listener. The old pain isn't twisting your thoughts into blame or vindictiveness. You feel more mobility in your body and attitude, and it's helping you to put yourself forward more and to speak from your heart. The roots you deepened help you to stand calm in the places where you used to flip out. You might even feel a sense of gratitude for the experiences that have rendered you so much more vibrant and chill.

You have grown. Genuinely.

But then . . . perhaps a project fails and your survival fears kick in. Or an old injury flares up, and some bleak thoughts distract from your confidence in healing. Or someone close to you makes a gloomy prediction about your future that's based on your past, and you are ohhh-ffended. Don't they know how far you've come?

And you think, *I already did the work—why am I getting this again? Why the repeat, the trigger, the flare up?*

"All the gods, all the heavens, all the worlds are within us."
    –Joseph Campbell

There are a few reasons that lessons repeat themselves.

The obvious reason a lesson circles back: we haven't learned all there is to learn from it. It's simple. We need another round to really absorb the teaching. You're undoing (literally) eons of social and psychic conditioning, so go easy on yourself.

The ego-self isn't in favor of evolving. We've got the free will to be resistant, and some of us can turn stubbornness into a profession. We resist Forgiveness—of ourselves and others. Or we distract ourselves with shallow things—surface relationships, entertainment, accumulations—in order to avoid feeling pain, which only delays our joy.

In which case, our Higher Self will intervene with some extracurricular activities to get our attention. *Holding back on your Love, are we? Playing small and denying your connection to the Universal Mind? Well, let me introduce you to a life-threatening situation to open up your heart flow. Avoiding healing that underlying condition of fear? Then how about an accelerated program in courage?* And we keep going through emotional boot camp until we come over the wall with a braver heart.

When we wake up to the futility of resisting life, we become more spiritually mature and agile.

And spiritual maturity wants to go all the way in every aspect of life. You'll want to have deeper conversations. You'll want to reveal more layers. And you'll figure out that our evolution is unending. And rather than feeling exhausted by or terrified of that fact, you'll get excited by being an eternal student.

> "The biggest embrace of Love you'll ever make is to embrace yourself completely. Then you'll realize you've just embraced the whole universe, and everything and everybody in it."
> –Adyashanti

Each of us is simultaneously superconsciousness, consciousness, and unconsciousness.

The subconscious mind is like a repository of impressions and suggestions living in the psyche. These are our "unchecked" thoughts . . . our conditioning and programming. The subconscious = our conditioning.

The unconscious mind is the energetic receptacle that holds fears and desires. We may only be somewhat aware of those fears and desires. These desires can drive us in all directions until we finally look deeper into the "why" behind them. Making the unconscious conscious is the healing work of one's lifetime(s). This is how we find the Light buried behind the shadows. The unconscious = the content that's driving us.

The conscious mind is the day-to-day rational, thinking mind that discerns and problem solves. Most mystics believe that about five percent of the human psyche is conscious. The conscious mind = our true awakeness.

The superconscious is the Unified Field—the all-inclusive, expansive, all-knowing awareness! This is considered the "holiest of all foundations," where flashes of deep insight, or abstract knowing arise. The superconscious = the Universal Mind.

And that's why we can be a sage in the morning, composed and ever-so-helpful to humanity. And the very same day . . . we can feel like an emotionally needy nutbag. And we think to ourselves, *I was queen of my own mandala at 10:00 a.m., and now I'm a needy nutbag.* S'okay, babe, you're revealing and healing more and more layers. This is the work. We're expanding our awareness of the multitudes that we contain.

The pain you may experience today does not invalidate yesterday's healing. The healing was real, and it's helping you become more conscious of what's beneath your surface. Maybe tonight you'll dig deeper, and you'll find something glorious or lopsided.

We're both static and moving every moment, living and dying. We are pure Light, and we cast shadows. Parts of us are ramping up their resistance before they come into balance. There are places in us where we are bound and blind. And there are places where indestructible Light beams shine. We are multidimensional and interconnected beings, and so our healing will never be a linear process.

Even when you think you're stuck, you're still connected to a highly dynamic world. Everything in the Universe is continually shifting in response to everything else in the Universe.

You are always changing. Everything around you is always changing. Our constant changes are interacting. That's why healing for one is healing for many.

Responsiveness and flexibility are great healing methodologies. So the wellness treatment or philosophical mindset that's been working so well for you for months, or for millions of people, might be due for review.

We don't heal in a sequential way, like "I dealt with my childhood trauma, and then I recapitulated some high school drama, then I processed my serious relationships, then analyzed why I was single for so long, followed that up with working out my issues in marriage, then I healed from divorce, and finally I realized everything happens for a reason, and it's all meant to be, and . . . SCENE."

You can let go of the pressure to be at a certain point of success by a certain stage of your life. That's all fabricated social structure. You are not a train on a track with a schedule. Instead . . .

Consider that you're a solar system. (This is more than a metaphor. We are made of the same stuff as stars, and our psyches pulse with the energies of the planets.) Within you is the polarity of the sun and the moon. There are new idea-stars being born next to dying thought formations. There are black holes of grief and spectrums of Light. There is mystery. There are infinities.

With all the possibility and perfection of the Universe, each of us is bound to discover that we are overflowing with Love and full of emptiness. We are a Soul with a human name. We are the consciousness that can observe both its consciousness and its unconsciousness. There are bound to be some beautiful contradictions.

"People who hold the contradictions and resolve them in themselves are the saviors of the world. They are the real agents of transformation, reconciliation, and newness."

    –Father Richard Rohr

We can accommodate grief and hope and sublime thankfulness all at once. Holding various emotions is not "crazy person" stuff, it's a divine capacity—a solar system with all kinds of planetary energies.

You can be penetratingly wise in many situations. With certain life assignments and people, you shine like the sun! And then some comet of resentment or disgust will come whipping through your atmosphere. And it's not that you're regressing. It's just time for that energy to come to the forefront, to be on your radar—and maybe to burn itself out.

Sometimes, the dying formations within us will require a lot of our attention. And we'll have to press pause on being a super-conscious member of society, so we can fall apart over the weekend or feel our fears in the company of people who Love us high and Love us low.

And then—it could be just minutes from now—you'll do something so spectacularly Loving and luminous that you'll even surprise yourself. The emotional release has made room for more Light. And it's like finding a new star in a familiar sky . . . inside of your heart.

Healing Cycles

Most of us are going to deal with the same cluster of emotional issues over a lifetime. Don't let that bum you out—it's good news. This means that we have the opportunity to heal *very deeply and thoroughly*. And we advance. You could think of it as getting to Love one person more fully, year after year—and what a gorgeous gift that is. Focused learning, usually in the form of repeated lessons, takes us through layers and levels of experience. We are mastering living and Loving. Life force and Love are always present, we're just honing our skills to find and elevate them—in all situations.

"All things in moderation" also applies to healing. Mercifully, our Soul guides us to revisit certain issues when we have the capacity to better handle them. "Handle them" is a relative term of course. Because when we're feeling like we're losing our minds or we're stressed beyond our previous comprehension, we probably won't think we're handling it all that well.

But in fact, we're meeting the healing with all the tools we have at the time, and we're being given the opportunity to become more agile with them. Maybe we learn to surrender even more. Or to confide in a new person. Or to hold the problem in ourselves just a little while longer before we seek outside input.

When we look back on our stormy passages, we might see that things were in perfect placement to help us weather the storm: a place to stay, a job to support us, or the spiritual resilience to help us trust the process and the will of the Higher.

Resources can miraculously emerge from the sidelines. We see the depth of someone we've been underestimating. Or we might wake up to the good fortune that we've taken for granted. Like a brother who, come to think of it, has never once let us down. Or a miraculous body that, despite the strain, has carried us and our babies everywhere. Or a sun that keeps rising.

The Soul exists outside of the mainframe of time, so all of its timing is divine. Maybe the emotional blockages that you dealt with years ago are circling back because you've become more courageous and adept at shadow work. It's not because you didn't finish the job way back then. *You've truly grown*, and the pain is back to be blessed—and finally released. When a familiar sorrow revisits you, receive it as an indication of your increased radiance and healing abilities.

On the nonlinear healing trip, you might notice that **your insights come in direct proportion to your Lovingness. The more you give and receive Love, the more Truth (and nontruth) you'll be able to recognize in all areas of life. Love is the ticket to the Universal Mind.**

You might realize that someone in your past never really "loved" you like you once thought they did—and you're really okay with it. We're all doing the best we can with what we've got.

You might actively allow painful associations to surface—and meet them with Compassion. In fact, you go looking in the dark to see what needs your Love and grace.

You'll understand that you're hugely responsible for creating your reality. And most days your enthusiasm will eclipse how daunting that can feel.

Chapter 3

WE ARE
SOUL-POWERED

Our personality isn't calling the shots, our Soul is.

HEALING HAPPENS WHEN we let our Soul, the Higher Self, take the lead to direct our words, thoughts, and actions. This is what it means to bring heaven to Earth.

Hermetic philosophy asserts that "God neither punishes, nor protects, nor rewards."

If you grew up in organized religion, this concept is a mind-blower. Most major religions—and many neuroses—revolve around the belief that there's a Higher Power outside ourselves that's keeping score and dishing out penalties for our good and bad behavior.

Paramahansa Yogananda dismisses that too: "Man should blame no one but himself for his troubles. God doesn't reward or punish anyone. Suffering is caused by the misuse of one's own free will. God has given us the power to cast him away or to accept him. God doesn't want us to suffer, but he will not interfere when we choose actions that lead to misery."

Buddhism also echoes this. With no central "God" figure to worship and all emphasis on awakening from the illusion of separateness, Buddhist perspective doesn't see an outside authority holding the scales of right or wrong. It sees karma—cause and effect—in our own hands.

And this aligns with the teaching of *A Course in Miracles* that espouses that there is actually no sin—we rest in wholeness: "Your holiness reverses all the laws of the world. It is beyond every restriction of time, space, distance, and limits of any kind." There are mistakes based on flawed perception, but those mistakes can always be corrected with Love—which always returns us to our awareness of wholeness.

If God does not want us to suffer, then who's bringing the suffering that we find all too real? The Soul's delivery service.

The Soul is always moving us toward expansion.

Expansion often reorganizes or obliterates previous structures and shows us new capabilities we could not have even imagined from our smaller point of view. The Soul's objective is to free our life force and increase our oneness awareness.

The Soul works on behalf of Divine Love. It is always pulling us toward our True Nature.

The Soul abides by the universal law of balance. Everything has to be brought into harmony.

The Soul's mission, should you choose to accept it, is Radiance. It helps to turn suffering into Light, consciousness.

Who punishes us? Our own mind with illusions of "us versus them" and separateness. And we can turn to Higher Source to help heal our minds.

Where does reward come from? Love is its own reward. And we can rest in knowing that we are Loved and made Loving by Creation.

What is our protection? Unity Consciousness. And we can give our hearts to the Divine for safekeeping.

> "We need to bury once and for all those fear-and-punishment scenarios
> that got programmed into so many of us during our childhood.
> There is no monster out there; only Love waiting to set us free."
>   –Cynthia Bourgeault

Free Will

Every single one of us is in a cell in the body of Mother Earth. She's THE Mama. And in this way, we're governed by Her energy. And Her consciousness is interplanetary. Everything in the cosmos is interconnected.

We're influenced by planetary cycles, much like the weather has an influence on us. It rains. We can choose to be miserable or just fine with it. We could get an umbrella, we could dance in the downpour. We have the free will to choose our response to all external influences.

You can choose the energy that you want to conduct through your life—in all circumstances. That's the best use of free will. Intend it and be it. Focus your heart-mind on a virtue and invoke its qualities into your thoughts, words, and actions. This is vivacity—bringing thought to life, vibration into form.

No one outside of you can energize your thoughts for you. There are truly gifted healers who can help ease your pain. But it's you that has to be open to receiving and assimilating that healing and carrying forward. There are great and illumined beings on this plane and beyond. And true enlightenment deserves all respect and homage. But the day of the guru is over.

No one outside of you has power over you. No one. Ever. You choose your response or reaction. More importantly, you choose the state of heart-mind that informs your response or reaction. Our application of free will—not circumstances, or karma, or the weather—directs the quality of our lives.

> "You will live in excuses and victimhood until you understand freedom permanently by taking full responsibility for your own life."
> –Rev. Michael Bernard Beckwith

My happiness and health are up to me. My life and death are up to me. On the surface, things may look random. I may look like the doer or the "done to." But I trust that my Soul is orchestrating her higher plan. I have turned to Source to file complaints about some of the events of my life, and I have begged for mercy. But I know that when I surrender, I can sometimes glide through the challenges. And when I ask for guidance, I get it.

May it become clearer to each of us, every day, that our Soul is working in concert with Source to direct our course. God's generosity is almost inconceivable—that we are *breathed through*, that we are animated, protected, blessed to know Love at all times, no matter what we do or do not do. So then . . . are we not honor bound to meet that life force with action? Actions for our happiness and health. Creation gives us existence and every opportunity to choose Love. We'll hit it. We'll miss it. And when we point our free will in the wrong direction, we'll learn the definition of mercy. Every breath is a new opportunity to get back into alignment.

Praise Creation by making Loving choices.

We have our free will, and we have our innate holiness. When we use our free will to honor our True Nature, we're in the flow of Loving Kindness. So you can kindly tell your fear-mind that you're in charge. (Emphasis on kindness.) And that you're going to navigate your life according to the principles of Love. This is what it means to direct your own course.

When we break those cycles of overdependency and/or being overly influenced by outside forces, there's a kind of pliancy that we have. All those spaces that we once filled with confusion and pain actually become buoyant and free. We level up.

Eventually you realize that you're in charge of noticing that life is really in charge.

Chapter 4

BLESS + RELEASE

Retelling old stories can hold us back from healing.

I'VE HAD PLENTY OF THERAPY. Jungian therapy, Gestalt therapy. A Jewish Buddhist psychotherapist. Most of my girlfriends have had a ton of therapy, which means I've gotten therapy by proxy: "So what did she say about him projecting all that onto you? Oh my God, brilliant!" For that matter, a bunch of my friends are actual therapists, coaches, healers, or facilitators, and I trained some of those facilitators myself. I'm covered.

There's been heaps of recapitulation and reclamation in my personal processing. I have cried, talked, and tapped it out. And with the exception of one very cranky counselor who I'm sure was projecting her unresolved issues onto me and accusing me of transference (see, this is the shit you say after you've had a lot of therapy), I'm grateful for every single hour doing the work that helped free me to Loving awareness. Some very skilled mind-knowers have guided me through the darkest passages of my life, and I'm indebted to them.

When we stay attached to our experiences, we can create suffering. So the healing inquiry is: **Are you willing to give over one painful experience— and the suffering that came with it—to your heart for healing?** Just one? And then another and another? Bringing each experience up to be accepted and completely Loved? So that it can be fully released?

The most sincere healers guide you to fully examine your woundedness—its origins and impacts—and to free yourself of its origins and impacts. We dive into the watery realms of past pain, and we reclaim the parts of ourselves that were dislodged by the floods of tragedy and trauma. And we resurface. More whole and more buoyant. Ideally, we keep flowing downstream with our lives. *We move on.*

But the shadow self finds those old murky waters of pain so tempting. And it will send us back, unnecessarily, to stir up old memories. We keep talking about our painful events. On and on with the retelling. We turn the trauma into a main character in our life's theater. Somehow, we're always finding subtle or overt ways to reference the pain in our conversations.

We impose past story lines on what's playing out in our current life. We might talk about how the new, challenging person in our life is a repeat pattern of someone in our family of origin. *She's a replay of my mother. This is the "father wound" all over again.* And yes, Psych 101 will tell us that we repeat patterns until we become more conscious and break the cycle. The wounded self Loves to re-create what's familiar—even if what's familiar is unhealthy.

But we can get trapped in the analysis merry-go-round. We keep looking at our present through the lens of our past. We walk through the world, through our relationships, asking, *How is this a reflection of my past?* And that's an incredible disservice to our healing and the opportunity in front of us to Love.

Let's say your father was absent, so unconsciously, you married someone who's out of town for work a lot and it's a source of pain—and healing—for you. Maybe your sister stole your boyfriend in high school, and now you're in a business partnership with someone who steals the limelight. Those old patterns may, in fact, be playing out.

On one level, it's productive to make the connection between past pain points and what we've created in our current life. (Notice I used the term "created" and not "attracted." I think "attracting" is more passive sounding than how manifestation actually works. Created feels more . . . dynamic and responsible. We like to think that we "attracted" that bad character, but that we "created" some good fortune. We're creating *all of it*.)

Back to how our past shows up in our present . . . Seeing what we're creating is brilliant self-responsibility. It's a means to empowerment.

But! There's a shadow side of correlating our past with our present life. We keep digging up what we've laid to rest. And when we do that, we're reenergizing that old pattern. We're reinforcing the old form. The retelling of those painful stories can hold us back from healing.

> "We do not heal the past by dwelling there.
> We heal the past by living in the present."
> –Marianne Williamson

Perspective informs our reality. If we choose to perceive people as repeats of our past, then we'll keep repeating the past. We can choose to let someone be who they are for us today, not a hologram of yesterday's issues.

Oversimplified Instructions on How to Let Go of the Past

Identify the wound. Where do you feel restricted, weak, or incapacitated?

Identify the impacts of the wounding. How does the woundedness affect your thoughts, words, actions?

Apply the medicine of Forgiving and Loving Kindness—for yourself and for others.

Leave the past in the past. See people and events of today with a Loving gaze. Which is to say, let Love dissolve your doubts.

Letting Go vs. Cutting Cords

If you've done some metaphysical homework (of course you have—you're here), you've probably come across the idea of "cutting energy cords" with people and places. We "send all that energy back to its source and cut-cut-cut those cords!" That practice can be a powerful remedy to imbalances and protecting ourselves. But . . . sometimes . . .

If you're in an emotionally volatile space, it can be difficult to dissolve energetic ties with people you're angry at or a situation that felt wounding or hurtful. *The "cutting ties" gesture itself can have an underlying aggression.* And that will just generate more angst—which is just another energy hook, more of the same story. **You can't let go of something that you're aggressively trying to let go of.**

We want to *gently and thoroughly let go* of all of the residual scars of a painful connection or event. Your part in the pain, their part in it, the pain in the middle. The pain over the pain. And then we offer it all up to be transformed into a higher vibration—which is how we create Wisdom. With the help of the Divine, we refine our suffering into Light.

We don't want to approach this as a "cutting away" or separating from our sorrow. It's about turning to the Divine with our pain and being healed through that connection.

Ultimately this is about identifying with our expansive nature, instead of feeling constricted. Constriction grips. Expansion lets things flow. And when we're expanded, we open ourselves to receive more healing and blessings.

Nothing leaves us until we thoroughly Love it.

We can't curse it to release it. We can't attack it to release it. That only creates more clinging and pushback.

Bless it: *Thank you for what you taught me. May you be free.* Then whatever it is—a relationship or a painful thoughtform—gets what it's always wanted: some Love. And then it will go on its way.

BLESS + RELEASE

BLESS + RELEASE

BLESS + RELEASE

BLESS + RELEASE

BLESS + RELEASE

BLESS + RELEASE

BLESS + RELEASE

BLESS + RELEASE

BLESS + RELEASE

Chapter 5

YOUR TRUE IDENTITY

**How we see ourselves and interpret the events
of our lives is what creates suffering or fulfillment.**

HEALING IS . . . making the transition from an ego centered to a heart centered life.

HEALING IS . . . learning how to be Loving. We become more Loving as we wake up to the true nature of life—which is Love itself and being our unique expression of that universality.

HEALING IS . . . identifying as inclusive Love. It's the journey from seeing ourselves as "small and separate" to recognizing that we're each a holy and essential part of the Divine Plan.

●

We're here—on the planet at this time—to heal, to embody qualities of the heart, *virtues*. A New Earth emerges from higher states of consciousness. We're evolving from fragmented personality identifications to more whole *beingness*, from holding grievances to generous Compassion, from standing in opposition to a unity that corrects all imbalances.

The Earth plane is a mashup of individualized karma, collective conscious-ness, and divine ordination—and it's all up for massive transformation. We can feel the shifting happening within our psyches, our nervous systems, and our relationships. It's playing out on the world stage. It feels both inter-nal and assigned. Pressurized and enlivened.

How do you move steadily through an epic shift for the human race? How do you do what needs to be done for your Soul's work? And for the next generation? How do you steer with Love when you're dealing with polar-ized personal conflict and a world that looks like it's out of control?

Focus on what YOU have the immediate power to control:
how you perceive yourself.

We stop the outer wars by bringing peace to our inner battle.

Identification causes suffering. Essentially, this is the first teaching of the Buddha. I'll put a finer point on it: *Misidentification* causes suffering. Misperception. An inaccurate conclusion of what we are.

How we see ourselves and interpret the events of our lives are what creates suffering or fulfillment. Do you see yourself as the wound or the healer? The past or the present? Alone or complete? Competent, capable, chal-lenged, doomed, blessed, supported?

Misidentification is: *I am my personality traits and my body. I am my career, my nationality, my reputation . . . my thoughts, my beliefs, my feelings. I am this "self."*

Truthful identification is: *I am pure life energy. I am a Divine Being. I am a Soul. I am a ray of the Light of Creation. I am you and you are me. I am the Eternal Loving Presence. I am one with the Universe. I am Divine Love.*

Identification as Divine Nature, as our Soul, allows our consciousness to expand. To even entertain the concept of being innately divine raises our frequency. *Just think about being higher energy and you generate higher energy.* This is the holiest use of the mind.

When we are conducting higher energy frequencies, virtues such as Love, Compassion, and harmlessness, we begin to dissolve our lower, fear-based energies. The higher subsumes the lower, and everything gets lifted into Loving awareness.

When we understand that we're divine energy beings and every single one of us is here to help humanity ascend to higher levels of Love, then our vanities and judgments seem . . . as petty as they are. A lot of what the personality gives power to is inconsequential and meaningless. When you know that you've incarnated to shine your eternally inextinguishable Light, does it really matter what people think of you or the car you're driving? Not so much.

How does a divine perspective work when a problem surfaces? Let's say you have a painful physical challenge that you're working to heal. The pain occurs. And before you choose your reaction to the pain sensation, you breathe into your heart and ask yourself, *What am I identifying with?*

Are you seeing yourself as the pain in your body? You're bigger than any physical pain sensation. Are you the body that's holding the pain? Your energy extends far beyond your organs and skin. Are you the brain that's firing pain signals? No, that's just your biology. Are you the mental mind that's chattering to you about pain levels and remedies? Those are thoughts and feelings—and you are most definitely not your thoughts or feelings.

You are the consciousness that's observing the thoughts, feelings, and physical sensations. You're the Eternal Loving Presence that's witnessing your current personality and body having a particular experience.

And that means that you can use your consciousness to transform the pain into healing. **You are not the wound. You are the healer.**

So! When any type of pain occurs you can think, *I'm Jane, and I'm sad and scared, and this hurts.* Which is probably how you will feel because you're human. Hold those feelings ever so gently. But keep your energy moving toward your heart center. You can make a choice at that moment to stay stuck in the limited identification, or you can breathe into your heart and remember that "I am the Eternal Loving Presence." And that means you have a universe of resources to draw on.

Or you can keep believing that you're just Jane.

Perspective Shifts Energy

Di·vine, adj.
: of or relating to Spirit, God
: extremely good; unusually lovely
: exalted, heavenly, celestial, glorious,
   sacred, blessed, all-powerful, holy, eternal

Maybe you're in a tough place emotionally speaking. You could be aware of it just sitting in your car or being in your living room, feeling that binding sensation of loss or dread of confrontation. The despair is a real experience. Just like the clouds that are really moving through the sky.

You can think one of two things: *I'm a small human in (inside of) despair.* Or . . . *I'm a spiritual being with despair passing through me.* You're not invalidating the heavy emotions, but you're reframing who's experiencing them and how. You can see yourself as bound by the emotion. Or as a strong container for the emotion.

Waking up from life-limiting identifications is the liberation that our Souls want for us. Instead of seeing our challenges as curses, we can see them as portals to Radiance. You can be awake to your sadness or frustration. You can regard your body as a conduit of Love rather than a cage.

You can sit in your pain, or you can sit *with* your pain.

This is the difference between seeing yourself as a flashlight or a Light ray streaming from the sun, as insignificant or as connected to Source.

When we see ourselves as Divine Beings . . . we stop craving fulfillment from sources outside of ourselves. We feel more empowered, capable, and whole. We play for Team Life Force. We know that we are fueled by the same prana that grows sequoia trees and emergent galaxies. And our memory returns us to sensing that we have never been, nor will we ever be, alone. Not ever.

For context, **"Divine Being": pure energy force. Soul. The frequency of Love. The vibration of Light. A perfect formation of energy particles progressing through the Universe. Limitlessly creative. Infinitely blessed. Sacred.**

When we see ourselves as Divine Beings . . . we stop identifying as broken, or defective, or behind. We stop letting our old stories direct our visions of the future.

When we see ourselves as Divine Beings . . . we slow the pendulum swing of pain and pleasure. We stop pegging ourselves into good or bad associations, as the victim or the vanquisher, as worthy or unworthy.

When we see ourselves as Divine Beings . . . we are not the diagnosis, or the prognosis, or any kind of prediction whatsoever. You are not what people think of you. You're probably not even what *you* habitually think of you.

When we see ourselves as Divine Beings . . . we know that we are most certainly not our past. We're no longer the issues, the patterns, or the scars we've accumulated. We are not the time we think we "spent" or the time we wish we had left.

When you see yourself as a Divine Being, you are the Greater Awareness that is aware that it is both aware and unaware. *You are the healer.*

Okay, let's review:

When a problem arises, what will you ask yourself?

This:
What am I identifying as?
A small self or my Higher Self?
My thoughts or my heart intelligence?
My defenses or my natural openness?
As behind or awakening?
Challenged or Divine?
As the storm clouds or the infinite sky?

A Metaphor For Your Soul

You are the Soul that owns the house you live in.

You have a house. You live in it. You decide what you bring into the house. You are the owner of the house.

The house is the analogy of your body. You are the Soul that owns the house. You own and care for and direct your body. Your house does not dictate to you. You control the contents and exterior of the house—your body.

The furniture in your house is your emotions. You get new furniture, you arrange the furniture in different rooms of the house. The furniture doesn't control what you do in the house. Your emotions are the same—they don't control you, at least they shouldn't. Emotions are just furniture and objects that come and go from your house. You, the Soul, are in total control of whatever emotions—positive or negative—that run through your energy field. The more resilience we've created as a Soul, the less our emotions control us.

Okay . . . your thoughts . . . Thoughts are like the electrical wiring in a house. When the circuits are firing properly, the house runs well. It's the right temperature, the lighting works, the water runs. You are in control of your thoughts. Ideally, as the Soul in charge, you're resilient and heart centered, so you're choosing and energizing thoughtforms that are aligned with virtues—higher vibration thoughts. So this is a beautifully functioning home.

If your thoughts are destructive, divisive, hypercritical . . . it's like the electrical wiring in the house getting overloaded. Circuits can blow or get corroded. We can adjust the amplitude, reroute some new wiring, switch the breaker back on—just as we can always cleanse our energy field so our inner state releases the blockages and higher energy can flow again. And if we blow some circuit boards, we can call in an electrician, a healer, to restore the system.

You are not your house. You are not the furniture, the wall hangings, or the appliances. You are not the plumbing or the electrical system. You are the Soul, the owner and the dweller of the structure, the house. The "house"—your body—is a structure to help you do what you need to do in life.

You use your house to have people over—you are not those relationships. We all play various roles in life. Parent, sibling, friend, leader. We're not our roles. We are the Souls that have chosen to be bound in time and space through a physical, emotional, and mental form (energy bodies) to play our roles. And by doing so, we resolve karma and heal ourselves and help heal each other.

You
are not
the wound.

You
are the
healer.

Chapter 6

TRUTH -FULL

**The heart is the library of
all you'll ever need to know.**

TRUTH WITH A CAPITAL T is almost inconceivable within the limitations of the human mind. High masters have referred to Truth as the principle upon which all speculation is impossible, the Great Unmanifest beyond the Great Beyond, Boundless Immutable Essence.

How can we wrap our heads around those sweeping vistas? We can't. It's mind-blowing. But we can move deeper into the heart space to find the Truth. In fact, that's the only place to turn with such colossal questions.

The yearning to know our True Nature is an evolutionary impulse.

Who am I? Why am I here? These are the questions of an awakened life.

True Reality may be inconceivable from this dimension, but if we **relax with the mystery and dedicate ourselves to discovery, we'll move closer to our aliveness.** Relax and dedicate ourselves to higher understanding. Dedicate and relax with the unfathomable scope of existence. Relax and dedicate to goodness in our words and actions.

A powerful sage once told me, "Let Truth be the keynote of your life, in this and future lifetimes." The recovering New Age keener that I am, initially I took this as a research assignment. Find the Truth. Here I go! And I gorged on all the mysticism that I could.

How do miracles occur? If you heal me, does that incur karma? If my reality is a projection of my thoughts, is changing my thoughts to help people improve their lives a manipulative act? If suffering helps to generate the Light of understanding, how should I relate to other people's pain, and my own? How does one bend time under the influence of planetary energies? What does sacrifice for the collective mean in relation to personal gifts? Show me. Teach me. Tell meeee.

> "The secret to life is meaningless unless
> you discover it yourself."
>
> –W. Somerset Maugham

You can't find Truth outside of yourself, no matter how much you study or listen to teachings. You could climb Kilimanjaro to meet a great, miracle-working guru in a cave for the secret of life and . . . they can't give you the Truth. The Truth only exists within your heart—where the universal becomes very personal. We *awaken* to the Higher through our Earthly life. We tap the eternal by being right here, right now, with all that is.

Seeking Truth as an intellectual pursuit can often get in the way of the Truth itself. We collect so many philosophies and rituals along the way that we end up having to toss most of it so we can hear ourselves think clearly.

The intellect tends to create barriers to Loving presence. *My preferences. My culture. My goals. The data. The history. The forecast.* Clusters of logic and information that get called truth—when they're really just well-formatted opinions that discount so many other possibilities and groups of people. Truth posturing is the ego's theater. It happens at all levels and sectors of life, from medical school to our family feuds, religious agendas, and staff meetings.

Imagine looking into a cracked mirror. Splintered and incoherent. That's how the shadow self reflects information, in broken-up bits. The ego-mind can only see slivers of who we truly are.

So-called truth (with a small *t*) on the world stage is utterly unbelievable. Even with good intentions and firsthand experience, all human accounting has degrees of projection. And if greed and manipulation get into the mix, then it plays out like a bad movie. When we stop centering our lives around lies, we can be guided by universal Truth.

The world upheaval is pressing us to go inward.

Truth—the Unified Field of awareness, synonymous with Love—includes everyone and everything, all dimensions. We are each a drop of pure Truth in the ocean of Truth. Every day, even on your way to work or wondering how you're going to get through whatever challenge is surfacing, you are carrying within you the *Boundless Immutable Essence*.

And you're going to realize that you've had it inside of you all along. Eventually.

While the great Truth of existence is mind-bending, the commitment to it is life-changing. The heart is the library of all we'll ever need to know.

You want to know the Truth? Reduce input from outside sources. Consider letting go of the teachers and their texts. And for the Love of God, turn off the news. Be still. Listen. Just live and see what you experience.

Love and keep Loving.

This will require courage.

You have it in you.

Bypass on By

Spiritual bypassing is where you put a spiritual spin on a "negative" experience to avoid uncomfortable feelings.

But before we find the "gift in the pain," we have to face the pain in the gift.

Let's say that someone steals an opportunity from you. And in order to bypass feeling all the "not so spiritual" emotions of anger and betrayal, you give the event a cosmic interpretation. "Must be my karma. It's all fine." Hey, maybe you thief'd their camels in a past life and this is payback, but now is now, and until your feelings are addressed and integrated, things can't come into balance.

Spiritual bypassing can give off the impression that we're taking the high road. We can skate on the surface with positive thinking for quite a long time. But the true spiritual work is to wade through the ditch of dark feelings, to get all mucky and frustrated with them, and then to climb out and still choose Forgiveness and morality on the other side. It's the dirty work that builds resiliency and Wisdom. The heart doesn't repress anything. It gets in there to pay attention to what's really going on.

Feigning harmony takes us out of our hearts. It seems ironic. What we think we're doing in order to be whole actually creates more separation. And this is how spiritual bypassing can be so destructive. Obviously, there's suppressive behavior—and what's suppressed often erupts. But possibly more harmful is that spiritual bypassing categorizes everything as either spiritual or not spiritual. And that's like saying some of us are divine and others are not. Or that only some of our feelings deserve recognition, while the rest should be critiqued and relegated.

Suppressing and condemning our feelings creates chaos and pain. Everything under the sun—including our rage and discrimination—warrants our mindful attention. This is the practice of consciousness. To observe all that is. When we avoid our pain and our perceived shortcomings, we're delaying our awakening.

I know many committed spiritual practitioners (and I count myself in this) who devoutly meditated, belonged to a church, or followed a guru, and after years of considering themselves to be awake or more advanced, the bottom fell out. Their spiritual leader got called out for abuse, or they themselves got struck with an illness, or waves of panic attacks came out of seemingly nowhere. And that's when their real awakening began.

They started to peel back the layers of their practices—to see that their spiritual striving was motivated by a desire to "become" more spiritual, which is the biggest spiritual bypass trip that there is.

When our practices get pared down, our dedication can deepen. The Loving awareness expands. And after years of trying to allay our egos, we can make the most enlightened declaration yet. "I have an ego. So what?"

It's all church, and it all belongs.

●

See your anger—and choose to act on your Forgiveness.

Listen to what your fear is whispering in the background—and then choose to be brave.

Feel your shame—and claim your eternal innocence.

Being fully human is a spiritual transformation.

An Incomplete and Ever-Growing List of Terms for God + Soul

God

Spirit. Eternal Loving Presence. Source. The Divine Feminine. Creation. The Infinite. Universe. Life Force. Prana. Qi. Chi. The Great Mystery. The Unknowable. Atman. Brahman. The Four Winds. Shiva. The Divine. The Mother. The Father. The Holy. Father-Mother-God. Father Sky. Mother Earth. Source Code. Universal Intelligence. The Cosmos. Omnipresence. Omnibenevolence. Yahweh. HaShem. G-d. The Lord. The Absolute One. Creator of the Universe. Goddess. Celestial. Supreme Being. The Immortal. The Godhead. The Avatar. The Animating Principle. Breath of Life. Vital Spark. The All-Powerful. The All-Knowing. Higher Power. Transcendent. The Maker. Goddess. Most Holy. Pachamama. Allah. Sophia. Waheguru. Jah. Is-ness. The Void. All That Is . . .

Soul

Divine Nature. True Nature. Higher Self. Heart Center. Non-Self. Unified Self. Beyond Self. Spirit. Anima. Essential Nature. True Being. Essence. Ka. Atman. Core Being. Intuitive Self. Eternal Self. Inner Wisdom. Higher Consciousness. Angelic Self. Divine Origin. Hun. Light . . .

Chapter 7

HELLO, EGO!

**The gift of the ego is to
show us who we truly are.**

THE EGO. THE SHADOW. Unhealed self. Wounded self. Small self. Abandoned self. Unconsciousness. Subconscious. Ego-ing.

Love it all.

The ego is the unhealed part of us. Or more succinctly, the ego is the way our unhealed self acts. It's not an entity outside of ourselves, it's our creation. It's a way of exaggerating a sense of a separate self. It's a way of identifying as being apart from Soul, from Source, and from all other forms of life. It's a way of seeing ourselves as alone, and therefore in a hostile universe. And the ego acts like it wants to keep it that way . . . but it doesn't. Not really. The ego is looking for Love.

We tend to think of ego as arrogance and grandiosity. Bravado and flash. But ego behavior also shows up as meekly insecure and overly self-deprecating. It will play all sides to try to keep you out of higher-vibration states and experiences, like Acceptance and communion. Shadows can make us power hungry and ambitious, and they can starve us of our self-esteem and keep us quiet.

We tend to think of the ego as a villain that's not "really us," something apart from our sacred nature. But the ego isn't actually separate from us, it just likes to keep up that appearance. And it's not even really a "thing."

The shadow comes from the same source as the Light. It's not real, it's only a projection. But it has a divine origin. All shadows are cast by Light. Which is to say, the ego is a figment of your imagination, but you're the one doing the imagining. You are the Light source casting the shadows.

So while the ego is a false sense of "an alone self," it very much belongs to us. And rather than trying to tame it or leave it behind on our way to enlightenment, we need to accept it for what it is and let it finally come to peace.

Ego-ing

The ego is a behavioral pattern. It's *a way of thinking* that identifies with a way of being. It's either on the defense or the offense, but never in the heart center. So it's not so much that we have an ego, it's that we "ego" our way through life. Adyashanti has called this *ego-ing*. When we could be Loving, we're *ego-ing*.

Recognizing the ego as a behavioral pattern helps us to dissolve the image of the ego as being an enemy outside ourselves. When we see the ego as a way of operating instead of an external character, it helps us be more understanding and compassionate with it.

So when we're being a bit arrogant or too timid for our own good, what if, instead of saying, *That's my ego that I need to get in check . . . scold . . . tame . . .* we just say, *Whoops, I was ego-ing.* And we can get back to Loving.

The Purpose of the Ego

Darkness calls on us to bring the Light.

The gift of the ego is to show us who we really are.

Ego thinking resists life. It's anti-aliveness that dulls our sense of our limitlessness and vibrancy.

Ego actions are driven by a conglomeration of unloving thoughts, essentially.

We learn a lot through contrast. Death helps us appreciate living. Fear trains us in courage. The ego helps us return to communion with life.

The small ego-self is masterful at hide-and-go-seek. It hides what it doesn't want anyone to see while hoping that it will attract someone who finally sees it for what it is.

The ego is also a wonderful trainer in intimacy. As we go about our ego-ing—comparing and fearing and rejecting parts of ourselves and others—we're getting to know what it means to have our shadows revealed. And that's an amazing opportunity for Compassion and Forgiveness.

Ultimately, the ego is always crying for Love.

Healing Addiction

Ego behavior is addicted to fearful thinking. The shadow tells you to keep on doomscrolling. It tries to remind us how we've been hurt before and why we shouldn't trust again. Like misery loving company, the ego shadow is always recruiting another illusion or hurt to huddle with.

We're all familiar with the addictive nature of negative, fearful thinking. It's a form of imprisonment.

Now pause and think about how society treats its addicted members: like defective, second-class citizens.

That's how we tend to treat the addicted and entrapped parts of ourselves. With contempt. When what every addiction and its host needs to heal is Compassion, understanding, and hope.

Harm reduction is a public health philosophy that supports drug users by focusing on positive change, free of "judgment, coercion, discrimination, or requiring that they stop using drugs as a precondition of support" (as defined by Harm Reduction International). I think this brilliant approach can apply to anything. Essentially it addresses the paradox that fighting against a harmful thing (whether it's drug addiction or ongoing anxiety) can't be treated by punishing the person who's suffering. Harm reduction removes moral judgment and simply focuses on creating a less toxic environment in which health is possible.

This is how we create conditions for healing.

Speak kindly to the part of you that looks for reasons to be afraid. You will have to be consistent and insistent. Extend reverence to the addiction and it will be less tempted to go looking for fear to feed on. All rehabilitation begins with sincere connection.

Peace

Suppression creates energy back-up and, eventually, toxicity. If we deny our needy and greedy parts, they will only become more . . . needy and greedy. If we admonish our shadow, it only grows from that punishing attention. Conflict is fuel for more conflict.

Love doesn't want to go to war with the ego, or with anyone. But the ego wants to war with Love . . . even though **what the ego needs more than anything is . . . Love.**

Have you ever been near a wounded dog that's barking madly? Survival instincts, adrenaline, confusion, and the animal fends you off with viciousness. But what it really needs to do is befriend its rescuer.

Our wounded selves are the same way. *Don't look too closely at me . . . bark bark bark . . . Don't ask penetrating questions that might reveal what's underneath my facade . . . bark bark. Don't confuse me by giving me affection when I'm so used to rejection. Bark.*

But more than anything, the wounded self wants to be folded into the healed self. The ego wants to be integrated, not segregated. It will resist. It will keep telling you that you are inferior or superior. It will tell you that what the news is parroting is more important than your mental health. The small part of you will tell you to tame your ideals and keep your opinions to yourself—because if you aspire higher, your smallness will outgrow its container.

All fragments of life want to return to the source of life. Even the small self was birthed by something magnificent. Resistance remembers relief. And the darkness remembers the Light.

The Ego Feeds on Self-Improvement

"The shadow self invariably presents itself as something like prudence, common sense, justice, or 'I am doing this for your good,' when it is actually manifesting fear, control, manipulation, or even vengeance."

–Father Richard Rohr

The ego's favorite hiding place is in . . . you ready? . . . personal-development workshops. Self-helpers and spiritual seekers really know how to *strive*, and striving is classic ego-ing.

The myth of separateness and abandonment that imprints the human psyche keeps us on a merry-go-round of proving. Church and state have been capitalizing on our abandonment angst for ages. This is our daily environment. A globalized economic system (hello, capitalism) based on the expectation of endless growth and progress—whether you're a small business or a single mom.

It's by definition unsustainable. Nothing grows or progresses forever without cycles of growth-ripeness-decay. Yet we hold ourselves to the same expectations as sociopathic multinational companies: to show the shareholders (or our social media followers) how much better we are this year than last. It's madness—and this constant striving is terrible for the planet and the people who live on it.

Self-helpers and spiritual seekers also uphold the values of humility, unity, and Compassion. It's a lot of upholding. Then there are the charity donations and peace rallies and petitions. Spiritual circles are the perfect place for covert ego-striving.

Being on the path and doing "the work" appears to be anything but arrogant or self-serving. Philosophies of peace spoken softly. Self-sacrifice. And it all looks great in stretchy yoga pants. *I'm body positive. I'm a meditator. I'm journaling daily. I'm fighting for peace.*

All these actions and commitments can be sourced from one's heart, a bona fide outpouring of dedication to Love. And . . . virtuous actions can be puppeteered by a shadow self that's telling you that you need to constantly burn your bad karma. Or that you can float above it all because you're more evolved than your normie neighbor.

Same spiritual practice, different motivations. Virtues that become vices.

The shadow hides in plain sight, disguised as "love" when really, it's just keeping people away from the Love they want. I thought I got free from Catholic indoctrination. But actually, I just swapped the Ten Commandments for the concept of karma, and I went to town proving how spiritually meritorious I was to my energy workers and Goddess Kali.

What we often call self-development is sadly just that—more development of a limited self—when what the heart is calling for is fewer selfies and more Soul.

Becoming Unbotherable

We each have a persona, cultural inclinations, and bodies we want to take care of. We don't need to pummel the personality out of ourselves to be more "spiritual." Even great masters and mystics have their own flair. We can honor our upbringings, our accents, and our pleasures.

Our identity structures help us navigate for a while, but eventually, we are going to wake up and go to work for the Infinite.

The trouble comes when we over identify with "where we came from" and what does and doesn't work for us. We become hard to please. Botherable. Political. Separatist in subtle and overt ways. Too much clinging to our personal traits and we end up congested with opinions. This bleeds into our social media sphere too: a subtle pressure to stake our claims regarding world events, culture, aesthetics . . .

The shadow nature is always pushing us to pick a side and go public with it—and so we close our minds to the possibility that our opinions change. It's all the trappings of cancel culture.

The more attached we get to our individual preferences, the more alone we can seem. And then the harder we'll fight or contort ourselves to belong to a group. And then the more polarized we become. It's a vicious cycle of having "high standards."

If we require people and circumstances to behave a certain way for our comfort and happiness, we'll never know real intimacy. Or peace.

If we prefer perfectly clean, polite, progressive, and punctual, or if we require laidback, ready to roll, and bold . . . we're just setting up all sorts of qualifiers for connection and happiness.

Excessive demands that we place on the outside world are a projection of our harsh inner critic. If no one and nothing is good enough for us, we might have a driving belief that we are not good enough for the world. We're striving to be perfect, wanting everyone else to go along with such idealizations, and no one gets to be Loved for all that they are. This is how the inner war unfolds.

We can project our shortcomings onto others in an attempt to deflect responsibility for filling up ourselves. We might need everything outside of us to be clean and quiet to quell our repressed feelings of mental clutter and shame. If you don't feel good enough, no one and nothing will ever feel good enough to you.

We can miss out on so much Love due to excessive preferences and identifications. It limits the diversity in our lives. Vegetarians only, vaxxed/not vaxxed, just the conservatives, please be my religion, have equal levels of optimism or Armageddon-think . . . on and on. These are all polarizing points in a world that desperately needs to unite.

What if the most Loving people we've yet to meet are nothing like our small self wants them to be? They are bigger, deeper, wilder, more uptight, more foreign to our beliefs, and more generous than we let our minds imagine?

We're taught to control our outer environment, when really we should get in touch with what's going on inside of ourselves. All wars end within us.

Of course we can have preferences and standards and still embrace others. Standards are a form of discernment and Wisdom. The heart knows what's conducive to wellness. So the question becomes: What are we basing our standards of morality on? On social appearances? Or on Unity Consciousness?

How do all living things grow, thrive, and overcome disease? Not by walling off in a sterilized bubble but by adapting to the novel substances and circumstances that come its way. Trees that grow in windy places grow sideways if they must. Living things incorporate toxins, adapt, and reject aspects of them, and move on—all the better for it.

As we become more fluid with our Love and assumptions, we become less botherable. And then something beautiful, and sometimes unsettling, begins to happen. As we bend and open, our scared self begins to trust. And our spiritual immune system gets stronger. We become more immune to discontent and more magnetic to goodness.

Chapter 8

ANATOMY OF THE WOUNDEDNESS

Forgiving is the ultimate in taking responsibility for our own healing.

LET'S TALK ABOUT THE ORIGINS of our emotional woundedness and how it plays out in our lives. Very basically: We have a childhood. We get messed up in our childhood by people who never healed from their own childhoods and are just doing the best they can. Then our early history gets replayed in the dynamics of our adult lives—until we wake up and break the cycle. (I think most of us understand this phenomenon. If not, please consult your nearest psychotherapist.)

Psychology supports this theory. Apparently, women with physically abusive fathers are more likely to marry men who are physically abusive. We are drawn to familiarity, even if that familiarity is harmful and toxic.

So, we could deduce that the early, formative events of our lives could magnetize similar dynamics to us throughout our life. This is accurate. But it's not the whole story.

We don't repeat a pain theme only because of the early events of our life-time. We incarnate with the theme and magnetize our overall challenges and blessings. The Soul chooses the circumstances that will facilitate our growth. Another way to say this is that we're born with the themes that then get played out in our very early lives.

We have a preassignment to heal a preexisting wound. The Soul selects the Earth family, the Earth family gives us an opportunity to work through what we've been carrying around for lifetimes.

The Soul says, "Let's continue to work on healing this eons-old pain." And the Soul magnetizes to us the formative relationships and experiences that will give us all the healing material we need to work with—from suffering to experiences of euphoria, from our hardships to our talents.

Let's say that someone incarnates with a pain theme of abandonment. Then it could be possible that they'll be born into circumstances where they are abandoned in some way—precisely so they can come to the revelation that they have never been abandoned by the greater Divine. And that they can generate the devotion and steady Love for themselves. Which is what we all so naturally yearn for.

We get thrown into the abyss to find our solid ground.

We face our abandonment to realize that we are the Beloved.

We face rejection in order to fully accept ourselves.

We face injustices to reclaim our innocence.

The Wound-to-Healing Sequence

1. **Family.** Welcome to Earth. You're assigned a family or caregivers. Naturally, they fall short of your fantastical expectations of perfect Love and supportiveness. Because no human—not even our parents or siblings, biological or otherwise—can meet all our expectations. Sometimes the pain inflicted is intentional and beyond comprehension. Sometimes the harm comes from even the best intentions.

2. **Rejection.** Whatever the degree of our disappointment or heartbreak, we feel cast out of our idealized Love—on the outside of what we most desire. Which leads to . . .

3. **Repression.** Out of care for others or fear of touching into the pain of our rejection, we tend to repress the painful emotions stemming from our rejection. Which leads to . . .

4. **Shame.** Unconsciously repressing the pain of our rejection builds into a sense of shame. Shame for wanting more, for not being "worthy" enough, for our own emotions of resentment. Which leads to . . .

5. **Guilt.** Guilt for feeling ashamed about repressing the truth of our emotional pain . . . about feeling rejected by a family that didn't meet our idealistic dream of Love. And then . . .

6. **Separation.** Predicated on not getting the perfect Love we expected, we perpetuate the illusion that we've been abandoned by and are separate from Creation, our family, our Higher Self, and everyone else on the planet. Which is designed to lead us to . . .

7. **Forgiving.** Imagine what happens when we Forgive the people involved in our originating circumstances. I know this is a tall order for some of us. But just considering Forgiveness will bring us into the vitalizing energy of the heart.

We will heal the wound of rejection, the habit of repression, shame, guilt, and our separation anxiety and abandonment issues *all in cohesion*. Forgiving our families is the ultimate in taking responsibility for our own healing and wholeness. We go into the muck and fertility of our human roots, we face the hardship and blessings of it all. And we find out that the Life Source has been holding and parenting us all along, never to abandon us.

Chapter 9

LIGHT + SHADOW

To heal our Inner Child is the most powerful medicine.
All other healing is secondary to this—it's *that* important.

The Golden Child + The Needy Child

REFLECTION. Imagine that you have two children. One of your children is an incredible athlete. They are a winner, an achiever. They're confident, genuinely kind, outgoing. You Love being together. It's easy to be proud of them.

Your second child is quite needy and challenging. They require a lot of attention and care, and sometimes you feel resentful about that. Their bedroom is in the basement because they make a mess. They holler for you, and you sigh and head down to help them.

The golden child is our conscious self on a good day. Adaptable and self-aware. The needy child is our shadow self, hidden in our psyche.

It seems easier to Love ourselves when we're getting it right, when we're achieving and in our stride. We reward ourselves. We have energy to share. We become encouraging to others. We're golden.

We coast and check off our boxes. We forget about the sensitivities and particular needs that we keep in the basement of our psyche. And then, usually at the most inopportune time, the needy kid in our basement will bang on the ceiling for some attention. They send you a sleepless night or nagging fear.

But you keep focusing on your successful Olympian ways. And for the most part, it seems to be working.

And so your basement buddy sends up another signal. They're scared down there. This time it's a minor health hassle. You keep going. So then they knock harder, and the health situation might get more critical, or you blow a big opportunity, or you start waking up in a sweaty panic at 3:00 a.m. for weeks. This is officially a wake-up call. The needy child now has your attention.

What's unconscious wants to be conscious. And if it has to burn the house down, it will.

"Whatever is rejected from the self,
appears in the world as an event."
–Carl Jung

Subconscious Characters

The needy child in this analogy is another term for the Inner Child. The Inner Child is a symbol to guide us through our shadowlands. It's our deep sensitivity, our unhealed self that's crying to be tended to.

To heal our Inner Child is the most powerful medicine. All other healing is secondary to this—it's *that* important.

This is key to understand: your Inner Child is not a version of you when you were a kid. Working with your Inner Child isn't about going back in time. We can just let our Inner Child show us what it wants to show us today, in present time. They'll show you all the unhealed perspectives that you're carrying—and how to heal them.

Connecting with your Inner Child is a simple tune-in. Close your eyes and take a few breaths into your heart center and ask your Inner Child to come hold your hand. That's them. Imagine how happy you are to see each other. Overjoyed, there's so much Love flowing between you.

And then ask them, *What can I do to support you at this moment? What do you need from me?*

And listen. The answer is usually very simple and essential. My Inner Child usually asks to walk in the forest and hang out with people who make me laugh. She says, *Dance today. I Love yoga. Ocean, please. Lie on the ground. Oranges for breakfast. I need a nap. Cello music. Fresh air. Play.* She also likes soft clothes and the farmers market.

If I would have attended more to these beautiful life basics years ago, I'd have saved thousands of dollars in therapy and health care costs and possibly spared myself a very dark night of the Soul.

Now, when I overwork, or plow through the day, or don't speak from my heart, my subconscious sends me a worrisome mind loop or minor pain to get my attention to *please slow down and go gently.*

See the reframe there? Worry, mind chatter, body aches . . . all the inner dynamics that we tend to resist, judge, and criticize about ourselves are usually the subconscious asking for conscious attention—Love. We don't have to have deep engagements with our mind loops. We don't have to over-privilege our mental chatter or let our body pain hold us back from getting on with the day. The Inner Child doesn't need to derail our aspirations—but we can't ignore it or its message. Just notice, listen for a minute. Adjust and move on.

Communicating with your Inner Child is not an attempt to get them to mature or be more responsible. We meet the Inner Child where it's at, with absolute attentiveness and care. You listen to their needs and sometimes demands. They get to feel their feelings and be adored. You can let your Inner Child know that all they have to do is be themselves and relax.

It's not their job to worry about earning a living, or politics, or taking care of anyone. You're the grown-up, and *you've got all that covered*. Let them know that you've got them, and the Divine Mother has got you.

The same goes for the host of fragmented selves in our psyche. The militant, uptight taskmaster. The rebellious outcast with authority issues. The golden children AND the needy inner children.

•

"Everyone carries a shadow, and the less it is embodied
in the individual's conscious life, the blacker and
denser it is. At all counts, it forms an unconscious
snag, thwarting our most well-meant intentions."
   –Carl Jung

Shadows are full of projections and judgments. For example . . . sometimes we try to dress up our shadow with good intentions. Aka martyrdom, halo polishing. And then we judge others for not working hard enough to be of service to the world.

For some of us, our shadow is neediness. We criticize ourselves for being needy, and we toughen it up and try to become islands unto ourselves. And while we're soldiering on, we're slightly repulsed by people who we perceive to be needy.

If anxiety is in your shadow, then it might seem like everyone's a stress agent. If your shadow self always feels helpless, then the world is on a power trip.

See how this works? We loathe a quality about ourselves, and we overcompensate or reject what we judge as a defect. And we feel slightly hostile to that quality in others. Loathing within creates more loathing without. Unloved shadows manufacture more shadows.

Until we look into our shadow—our unconscious—and offer Love to what we find there, we'll be in the perpetual cycle of judgment.

●

Our shadow is the stuff that we tuck under, that we hide beneath all our distractions of workaholism and comparison and bravado. It's the stuff we're not dealing with. That's the basic definition: the shadow is the stuff we're not dealing with . . . yet.

Eventually we'll have no choice but to enter into our shadows. As the sage philosopher Joseph Campbell put it, "You enter the forest at the darkest point, where there is no path. Where there is a way or path, it is someone else's path." You're the hero, and the forest is your inner landscape.

> "All darkness vanished when I saw
> the lamp within my heart."
> –Kabir

You're going to find many varieties of fear within. Fear of loss, fear of rejection. The old classic: the fear of death. Some overgrown terror is a likely find. Terror like *Will I ever get what I most deeply desire?* And then more terrorizing with *If I get what I most deeply desire, will it be taken away from me?*

Eventually you start to get really curious about what's nestled in your shadow, about what's driving your thoughts and actions from below the surface. And more and more often, you'll ask yourself why you said certain things or behaved in a particular way. *Why did I say what I said in that interaction with them? Oh . . . that was my fear of rejection speaking.* Your curiosity turns inward. You turn to your Higher Self to observe your smaller self. This is the flourishing of consciousness.

And you can delight in becoming more aware—even as you identify all the gnarly, unflattering, rejected parts of yourself. And that's how you find the Light in the dark.

> **Light is in the fabric of all things.**
>
> **Darkness is only the absence of Light.**
>
> **The Light exists even in the dark.**

Acting Out

Our negative actions, those not-so-appealing behaviors, are just expressions of wounds that have not yet healed. Addiction, aggression, greed . . . it's just a wound trying to get attention from you and the outside world. And the best form of attention we can offer it is the Light of our consciousness. *I see you. I Love what I see.*

Hiding Spots

Overwork is one of the most popularized ways of avoiding our shadow. If we stay in motion, we outrun the anxiety underneath the surface.

I personally know this cycle very well. I used to overwork, because if I kept achieving by being of service to the world, then I was earning my keep on the planet. If I kept earning my keep, I could keep wishing for my desires to come true, and then I didn't have to look at the fear that I wouldn't get what I want. I didn't have to look at the questions around worth and deservedness that were underneath the desires. So I just kept working hard to get what I wanted. *I will be so good for God, God will deliver, because isn't that how karma works?* I thought. Nope. That's just a cover-up for unhealed wounds around "worth."

Shadow avoidance shows up in excessive ambition for money and status, accumulation of material things, addictions—dopamine hits from social connections on our devices, substances, or fixation on our roles and duties as "mother," "leader," "activist," "Christian" . . .

The all-time distractor from shadow work is the maintaining of shallow relationships. If we're not going deep in our key relationships, then we're not going deep into ourselves. Emotional and spiritual intimacy with others is the portal to our inner landscape.

All relationships are yoga. The interactions inevitably bring our repressed qualities to the surface. We can let our ego-mind pull our strings like a puppet. Or we can get curious and honest.

> **Here's the beautiful, glorious, good news: Where there's shadow, there's Light! Where there's pain, there's power. Where there's illness, there's the cure.**

●

Hello, Inner Child . . . shadow self . . . unhealed bits. I've got you.

This is how a conversation with my shadow self might go—usually when I feel agitated, or worried, or my authority issues kick up. I also talk directly to my Inner Child when I'm in any kind of physical discomfort since the unconscious uses the body as a megaphone.

I speak to the emotional or physical feeling that's come to the surface:

Oh there you are. Wounds in the shadow . . . Inner Child in need . . . helloooo. I see you. I see your fear. I see your shame. And you know what? I'm not judging you anymore. I'm going to embrace you. In fact, I'm going to listen to everything you need to say. (As hard as some of it is to hear.) So . . .

Unravel. Don't stop. Tell me everything. Even if you're spewing and sputtering, I'm going to focus my attention on you. Let my Love calm your nervous system. I'm your medicine woman.

I know it may be hard to trust, because I've neglected you in the past. I've plowed ahead when you needed rest. I should have eaten when you needed nourishment. I created relationships that weren't supportive. But I'm here now. 100 percent.

So, dear shadow self, do you need me to stop overworking so we can rest and be well? Okay. You need me to get into nature more so you can feel nourished and aligned? Okay. You need me to break up with situations that are insensitive to your deep sensitivity? Okay. I'm going to value your life with my Compassion.

You're in the dark, and my Love is the Light.

The Divine Mother has me, and I have you.

●

Lightwork

"Lightwork" is bringing the *unconscious* up to consciousness—to shine Light on what we've kept in our darkness and not fully Loved. Lightworkers are excavators.

Shadow work is about seeing the perfection of who we are, even with our faults. We all have ugly parts and unresolved problems. So then, how powerful is it to accept ourselves relentlessly? How powerful is it to continue to enter into our shadow tunnels while expanding our Loving awareness? To bring Light to the dark? It's miraculous, is what it is.

Shadow work is not about finding more fault with ourselves and making piles of our "good" and "bad" traits.

When we're hostile and abusive with ourselves, we're actually denying our shadow side. The harsh treatment just numbs the pain that needs to be healed. It's a pain pileup that can lead to more self-violence.

Your paranoia, your selfishness, your nastiest thinking, whatever you're keeping in the basement of your psyche, just pour Love on it. Seriously. Sometimes those fragments will flail and kvetch. Your neediness will get whinier. Your rage will screech. That's fine.

Your heart is immense. You've got space for *everything*. Inside the cocoon of Compassion that is your heart center, all the abandoned parts of yourself will metamorphose. **And the fears that tried to keep you from living will become the Wisdom that guides your life.**

Happiness

Not all characters living in our shadow are frazzled or demanding. There can be restrained beauties and geniuses just waiting for you to recognize them.

I was amazed to find a fragment of myself that just wanted . . . *to be happy*. Simple happy. Normal happy. It's the part of me that felt selfish and unevolved for desiring ease. She was buried under my activism and business projections, always in conflict with wanting to build a better world or to build a beautiful day for myself and my kid.

I was grinding it out for the cause and seeing that the world was unraveling in big, unprecedented ways. I was asking myself what my role was during this arduous, beautiful passage for humanity. And at the same time, balancing my health, motherhood, life partnership, and a high-productivity business. And then there was cancel culture, wokeness, awakeness, and watching some of my friends', family's, and Heart Centered members' lives get shredded by conflict and save-the-world considerations.

In a slightly confessional, exasperated tone, I said to my coach, Colin, "I just want to be on a beach, and be in Love, and not go to a protest march this weekend . . . and not feel guilty about any of it." Coach Colin is a Zen practitioner, so he asks really obvious questions that make me laugh-cry a lot. "How would it feel to be on the beach, Danielle?"

"Well . . . HAPPY is what." Colin waited for me to catch up to myself.

"Oh my God . . . You know what? There's someone in the basement of my psyche that just wants to be *happy*." All this time I thought my shadow was harboring my evil twin. But out stepped a version of me that said, "Would it be all right if we didn't try to reconstruct reality this week? I'd like to go for a walk and just be happy." Hunh.

"Contentment can be just as enlightened as your consciousness flying around the Universe," Colin counseled. He knows that I need to be convinced of such outlandishly simple ideas. So for good measure, he threw in "God *wants* you to be happy."

That very thought made me very, *very* happy.

The greatest revelations are always pure and simple.

Radiant Happiness + Shadow Happiness

Happiness can be a confusing term. There's a kind of happiness that's interchangeable with the vibration of joy. *It's a Radiant state of being.* Radiant happiness.

And there's shadow happiness. The fleeting emotional highs we get from stuff that's really not good for us. It's the one-too-many drinks or donuts kind of happiness. Retail therapy happiness. Hanging out with someone because they make us look good kind of happiness. The small self will reach for fillers and quick fixes and call it happiness. And it's a big setup for unhappiness.

Radiant happiness is a higher frequency. It doesn't come from filling a craving, it comes from the fulfillment of just being present. Present to how amazing it is to be more aware in this moment than you were yesterday. It's a no-matter-what kind of gratitude for being alive. It's a connection to your vitality.

Radiant happiness holds the neutrality of real Love. The heart is phenomenally flexible—it Loves no matter what. If you get some bad news? You can still sense your underlying Radiant happiness. Amazingly fantastically promising news arrives?! You know that the steadiness of your Radiant happiness is going to keep you from overwhelm or discounting the joy.

I was talking to a friend who was in the natural disaster of her life. Asteroids of family illness and mental strain were crashing toward her every week. She focused on the growth, on how her Love and Faith were in full force. "You happy with the progress you're making?" I asked her. "I am absolutely satisfied either way," she said in her dignified way. That's Radiant happiness.

Shadow Sharing

I've regarded "the Light" as an omnipotent presence that we all originate from. When I'm aware of this glorious Radiance, I have the image of a smaller me standing beneath a shimmering downpour—accessing something that's available to every single one of us. Just like we all soak in the sun's rays.

For a long time I conceptualized of "the shadow" as my own dark corner of the Universe, sometimes bumping up against other "darknesses"—like rain clouds congregating. But if the Light is a great presence that we each tap in to and express in an individualized way, then so is the shadow. It isn't "my shadow versus your shadow." The shadow is a collective phenomenon that we each tap in to and express in our own way.

So you could say that just as we each transmit the greater Light, we each transmit the greater shadow. It shows up in our judgments and divisiveness.

Bring Your Shadow with You

Every day is Bring Your Inner Child to Work Day. Your subconscious wants to be included in your life and carried along. Don't leave your insecurities at home when you go to your job. Bring them with you. They'll be less anxious that way. Bring your scared bits to your intimate interactions, that way they get the benefit of your connections.

And keep communicating with your shadows. It doesn't matter how illogical or outrageous your deep emotions seem. Hear the Wisdom and the madness. No silencing. No criticism. All Acceptance. **If you gaslight your unconscious, you will never have a truthful conversation with yourself.**

●

Whatever is healing for your shadow will benefit all parts of your life.

In our shadows, in our woundedness, hides our greatest opportunity to be whole—to be everything we were born to be. Our manipulativeness, our arrogance, our hostility, our addictions . . . they aren't irreversible personality defects or fractures in our spirit. They're just . . . behaviors that sit on top of, and sometimes override, our integrity.

The Gospel of Thomas gives us a powerful philosophical pillar for life: "If you bring forth what is within you, what you bring forth will save you. If you do not bring forth what is within you, what you do not bring forth will destroy you." Thomas isn't just speaking about the drawbacks of condemning our longings. He's calling us to lead with our Light, with our heart force, so that our shadow doesn't wreak havoc in our lives.

Everything wants to come back to the center of the heart—humanity's home base. The parts of ourselves that we outgrew and can't believe we ever were. The splinters of personality that we only bring out on certain occasions. The fears, the secrets, the afflictions we never talk about. It all wants to be re-homed by our Love.

Self-compassion is your brightest, most powerful source of Light. Use that self-compassion and shine it on your deepest pain, on the full spectrum of your pain—the pain that seems recent and the stuff that feels ancient.

Keep looking. Keep listening. And keep Loving what you find in the dark.

And *that*, my friend, is shadow work.

PRACTICE
Inner Balancing

> Engage with your unconscious in a daily, practical way:
>
> Put your right hand on your belly—the lower chakra for survival.
>
> Place your left hand on your heart chakra.
>
> And ask your shadow or Inner Child: **"What can I do to support you to come into balance?** I've got you. I am looking after you. I'm never leaving."
>
> And then listen with Love.

Chapter 10

FEARS + FRAGMENTS

The purpose of emotional pain is to get us to tend to unresolved issues and to unblock and generate our Loving awareness.

THINK OF THE EGO AS ONE BIG OPINION. I think in Latin it's called the Opinion Majoris. Opinion Majoris is of the mind that fear should run your life. Opinion Majoris then spawns a bunch of "opinions minoris" to carry out the fear thinking. Those minor opinions express themselves via fear-based beliefs about politics, and relationships, and humanity, and the future. This is all the ego really is, a large thought fragment that splinters reality into things that we think we should be afraid of or fight against.

We have to wrangle up and return all the minor fears to their operating system. And then we can bring the ego back to our heart to find peace. Becoming whole is the process of greeting our fragmented selves—and then eventually welcoming in the creator of the fragmentation.

When fear is floating around as a fragment and it's not included in our heart space, it will show up as pain or illness or as setbacks. So we don't need to look far to find where our fear-based ideas are having an effect.

Our life challenges kick up our unconscious and conscious fears.

What fears are being triggered by your struggles?

Fear-triggering is one of the functions of emotional pain. Pain brings unconscious energy to the surface that needs to be released . . . so we can become more of who we truly are.

The purpose of emotional pain is to get us to tend to unresolved issues and to unblock and generate our Loving awareness.

So . . . with a Loving gaze, take time to look at the fears that underlie your pain, illness, setbacks, and challenges. (This introspection can be life-changing.)

You can trace those minor fears back to a major fear that's usually a version of the fear of annihilation or abandonment. A terror that we won't be Loved and sustained by Source.

Love your fear. Do not confront it in hopes of "facing it down" or rising above it. And please don't try to crush it. First of all, your fear mind is not attacking you, it's trying to get your attention so you can show it some Love and calm down. Like that scared, barking dog on a chain, your fear only wants your attention because it wants your Love. Any response to your fear that is not understanding and compassionate is really just hostility, which will only jack up the fear.

Compassion breaks every vicious cycle.

Rather Than Forcing, Invite

Fear is not something to be "overcome." I know, I know, we think that process makes us stronger and more badass. But look, you can force yourself to cliff dive or you can *encourage* yourself to cliff dive. Force or natural magnetism. Different energies, even when applied to the same action, will have different psycho-spiritual outcomes. It doesn't matter what you achieved on the outside if you're still bound and contracted on the inside.

I posit that if you're standing at the edge of a cliff and you tell your fear to shut the eff up and you jump . . . that demeaning exchange is only going to exacerbate your underlying fear. That tells the subconscious Inner Child that it doesn't deserve to be heard, especially when we want to accomplish something.

The adrenaline high might make us think that we made progress. We take our outer achievements as evidence that we're making real progress. But we still haven't brought our fear into the Light. We just sucked it up and jumped . . . or kept playing our roles at work, or life hacking, or success chasing. Overriding our deepest needs.

Forced change doesn't create genuine or lasting change.

Let's go back to the edge of the cliff for that dive into the ocean. Your fear is chattering, "I could die. Worse, I could knock out my veneers. I'm going to turn around. Either way, this is going to be so humiliating. I can't." Notice that your fear is giving you some useful information. It's linking death with humiliation. You can unpack that later. You just breathe. Nice and rhythmically. Focus on your aliveness.

Now calmly converse with your unconscious mind. You could respond with "You're afraid of dying? I get that." And in that very instant, with just a second of caring attention, you just interrupted a lifelong pattern of rejecting your shadow side. What you did right there is an act of Loving Kindness that's about to change your brain waves. Please continue . . .

You don't need to give your subconscious voice an inordinate amount of airtime. You're in charge, and you're choosing to *consciously* live your life. After you hear it out, assure your subconscious that you've heard what it had to say and you're holding it close and that it's invited to go on this adventure with you. No fragments left behind. You're doing this *together*. And you could even say thank you to your fear for helping you to be more alert and alive. And then . . .

You fly.

●

We will keep going back for more pain until we realize that we are not the wound.

Let's say your pain theme is not being accepted for who you are. Maybe a parent pressured you to become more of this or less of that. Or you got teased at school for being some version of uncool or too cool. Maybe a relative lectured you about what they regarded as poor choices. Or one of your romantic partners let you know that they thought you were either too much or just not enough. (See how most of our learning comes through relationships?)

So you began to adapt to what people expected of you instead of drawing on your True Nature. And that adaptation may have become habitual. Depending on who you're interacting with, you might dial your energy up or down to try to get the Love and Acceptance you want in all of your relationships. *All of them.* At work, with your partners, with the barista you've just met.

Except . . . it still feels like no one really accepts you for who you truly are. And that painful story is the one that you keep rereading to yourself, over and over. And so you start tallying up the rejections: People who don't call back after the meeting. Getting passed over for the promotion. Your mom still doesn't get very excited about any news you share. Your bestie started drifting when you told her your theory on the New World Order. And you're not imagining it. You do indeed experience a lot of rejection.

You can see that you keep getting hurt or offended in the same way in different circumstances. And the more that happens, the more you think that you yourself are just unacceptable. Until eventually the weight of that recurring pain becomes unbearable. And it brings you to a breaking point, an emotional pit, or an extended dark night. And when you get on your knees to look squarely at that awful feeling, you see that it bleeds into every area of your life.

To stop the bleeding, you learn how to apply Compassion to your wound. Finally.

For a period of time—it might be a sabbatical or months of focused inner work—you orient your life around healing your pain theme. And as you let your Compassion be the compress to your pain, you realize that you are not the wound itself. You see that you are the source of the Compassion—you're the creative force.

You are not your backstory.

You are the story writer.

And you have a new story to write that looks nothing like your past.

It's the story of becoming whole.

Overprotective?

REFLECTION. Ask yourself: *What part of me wants to be safe?*

Is it your emotions, your physical body, your various beliefs?

Your Soul isn't concerned with safety. It exists as Light, so there's no threat of darkness or the unknown.

The desire for safety comes from the wounded aspect of us wanting to stay safely hidden in the familiar shadows.

But the shadow self doesn't actually need safety. Hiding is not helpful, it's actually detrimental. The wounded aspects of us need the energy of Love to heal. The shadow self needs movement and courageous action. It needs your joy and your vitality. THAT energy current is what's real and healing. Safety in the dark is just an illusion.

While the heart is always conveying that we're ultimately free and safe, the ego tries to talk us into taking more safety precautions. Security is what the ego-mind is selling. And what a scam. Because nothing is totally "safe." There are floods and surprises, walkouts and endings. And there's always death to look forward to.

The only reliable refuge is Loving Kindness—the heart center. It's the only guarantee of sanity and joy.

REFLECTION. **Consider the following big, deep questions—that only you have the answers to (every answer you have is the right answer for you at the time):**

- How can you accept everything that you bring up from your shadow?
- How can you stay present with everything that your shadow self reveals to you?
- How do you Love the habits and behaviors that you hope will just disappear?
- What will help you to heal your fragments and their circumstances?
- How do you integrate all of it to become more whole on your life journey?

Chapter 11

ACCEPTING YOURSELF

Acceptance is the ultimate openness.

SELF-ACCEPTANCE IS THE GATEWAY to life force. The mind relaxes from all the stories it makes up, our awareness unfurls, and we rest . . . in Love.

Self-acceptance is so counterculture that it upends the patriarchy, the matrix, and epidemics of self-doubt.

Self-acceptance is the most peaceful of powers.

Self-acceptance requires courage—the fortitude of the heart.

Self-acceptance will be the undoing of you. The undoing of identities that are terribly false or too narrow—even the spiritual ones or the socially applauded achieving ones. You will be called to unlearn heaps of dogma. You will be invited to Forgive the seemingly unforgivable and to abandon things that you spent a long time constructing. You will have to navigate in the world with fewer operating principles, fewer rules. **From law . . . to awe.**

Your self-acceptance may look like a rebellion or betrayal to others.

In accepting yourself, you may embrace the weight of the issues that you haven't fully dealt with. That Loving embrace will make the pileup much more manageable. You will unleash a kind of exuberance to keep dealing and unfolding.

Self-acceptance is fierce responsibility, a ruthless Compassion. And as you root into the center of your heart, where all things are included and revered, then you can relinquish all the projections that you put on the world—about who to be angry at, or who's even angrier than you, or who's brighter or righter. You see the power that's within you, and you no longer need to pretend it exists outside of you.

You will stand in front of a million messages of your so-called unworthiness, sandwiched between heaps of "right" and piles of "wrong," on top of your giftedness and glowing heart, and you will say, *I Love and accept it all.* You will do this regardless of how your idols live their lives or what the oracle said.

You will accept yourself, shadow, Light, and all the layers that reveal Truth.

Free of all the betterment traps, you will breathe so fully, so rhythmically now. And on your next deep inhale, you will be filled with the spirit of generosity.

When you accept yourself, there's so much to give . . . just by being you.

Unselfing

"The most terrifying thing is to accept oneself completely."

  –Carl Jung

We're here to unlearn, un-become, dis-believe, and de-program from any dictum that says we're less than divine. Liberated living doesn't require a permission slip from a guru or elder. It's between you and the God of your understanding—and however you want to live, God's going to understand.

In order to wake up, we need to have one singular intention: to wake up— to make Truth the keynote of our life. This requires us to **become intimate with our thoughts** so we can sift the Truth from the fallacies and move closer to our heart center, not further away from it.

> "This isn't a journey about becoming something. This is about unbecoming who we are not, about undeceiving ourselves. In the end, it's ironic. We don't end up anywhere other than where we have always been, except that we perceive where we have always been completely differently. We realize that the heaven everyone is seeking is where we have always been."
> –Adyashanti

Reverence

rev·er·ence, noun
: profound awe and respect, often Love
: devoted warmth, veneration

It's only Love that perceives Love. Hate doesn't look at a person and see their implicit beauty. Greed can't see poverty with Compassion. Only Love can see all there is to Love. The heart is our instrument of Truth. It sees clearly, and it radiates Love onto what it sees.

The ego-self has impaired vision—it's in the shadow, after all. **Anything that is not seen through the view of Love is inaccurate.** The heart looks outward with the sight that the Divine has placed within us.

Which set of eyes are you looking through when you see someone in a store, or on social media, or across from you at the dinner table? When we look at ourselves and where we're at in life, are we looking through the heart, or has our shadow self stepped in front?

When we stop thinking in terms of superior and inferior, desire and aversion, then the partitions around our heart come down. The mind erects those barricades to Loving awareness. And it's the mind that can take them down. When that happens, we see that we're in an open-energy field in which *everything belongs*. Nothing gets turned away. Not your neuroses or your grievances or your illnesses, not power struggles or world wars.

Love is always choosing to Love. It will always seek the Truth in people and situations. And it will go one step further by Loving—revering all that it finds.

> "There is nothing in this universe that may be
> treated with disregard or contempt."
>   –Anandamayi Ma

If you were to look at yourself with a Loving gaze, what would shift? What old, limiting stories would start to dissolve? What tightness would loosen? What would be Forgiven, relaxed, diminished, celebrated, more cherished?

The Loving gaze is reverent.

REFLECTION. Imagine being in awe of your doubt. Instead of talking down to your worries, you would uphold them with respect. *Wow, doubt, I get that you're telling me something. You really make me stop and pause, and remember my Faith. I see your service. Thank you for helping me get centered.* And as the doubt (or fear, or anxiety) is so respectfully acknowledged, it begins to settle down. All feelings calm down when they are welcomed in.

Picture what it would be like to show some respect to your shame. That's a big one. That shame-y energy that likes to hide in the dark corner hoping it never gets talked about. What if you gave it back its dignity? *Hello, shame, I see you. I get why you feel the way you do—totally understandable. I'm going to go on living, creating things I'm proud of. But you're welcome to stay while I get some work done.* And then, like Boo Radley coming out from the porch shadows, maybe your shame takes a step into the Light of Acceptance that you've so kindly turned on.

The heart feeds the invited guests and the party crashers. Imagine giving a warm greeting to one of your so-called rivals. Remember, you're seeing them with a Loving gaze, not competitiveness or hurt. So for that moment, you can relate to what you both might cherish, to why you're both trying to succeed.

Reverence is a Soul capacity. And the more we can meet our experiences with respect, the closer we get to the full power of our Soul. The Loving gaze transforms everything it sets its sights on.

●

"Much of spiritual life is self-acceptance, maybe all of it."
    –Jack Kornfield

Accepting yourself allows you to be more at peace with whatever is going on in your life and around you. It gives you a base of sanity and Loving Kindness to work from.

If you're friends with yourself, you can make friends with everything that's going on in your life.

Fear resists life, while life is everywhere shouting, "*Live me! Live me in your body. Live me in the freedom of Forgiving. Live me and swim me, and share me, and express me.*" And fear stays indoors, just to be safe.

Acceptance is the ultimate openness, one of the highest forms of Love.

Acceptance Is the Best You Can Do

"God said, 'Love your enemy,' and I
  obeyed and Loved myself."
    –Kahlil Gibran

When you're on the path of intentional awakening, the ego-mind can get really tricky. As we're diligently trying to inch closer to enlightenment, the small self will tell us that we're not enlightened enough.

When the voice that says you're not enlightened enough starts to come through, you've got to rush in with some self-compassion. The response is profoundly simple:

I'm doing the best that I can.

(Say this in the most Loving, affirmative, friendly tone. Because it's a statement of celebration.)

Are you doing the best that you can?

Highly likely.

And that's Divine.

Love it all.

No matter what.

And don't stop
Loving.

Chapter 12

ACCEPTING LIFE

Nothing changes until you accept it.
And to accept it is to Love it *as is*.

MAYBE YOU'RE IN THE HABIT of petitioning a higher power for assistance, for yourself, or on behalf of a Loved one, or for our hurting planet. It may be a quiet conversation that you have with your inner guidance every morning. Or a prayer. It could be a call to your most intuitive friend. Or your petition for help might be an on-your-knees plea to the Almighty from the bathroom floor at midnight. *Please, God . . . guide me, get me out of this, help them to . . .*

We want relief. We hope for mercy. We're asking for directions.

What if we look to understand the reason that something is happening before we ask for it to be changed? Like, before we order a solution, we first try to understand the problem. Knowing the root cause of something is how we find the best remedy.

What if we asked for a status report from Universal Wisdom before we appeal for mercy or to be rescued? We could press pause and inquire about what's going on. *Dear Life, why is this happening?* Or *Why is this situation on the planet? Like, really, why?* Not what your mind sees or what the news reports. "Why is this happening?" is a threshold question that takes us from dusk to dawn of awareness.

And maybe you'll hear some useful answers to this question that point you in the right direction for specific healing.

But the eternally truthful answer to "Why is this happening?" will always be the same: it's happening for your expansion.

And maybe that's all we can know at the moment. It's definitely all we really need to know.

Everything we encounter is for our expansion. The Divine is never indiscriminate, and its mission is singular and unstoppable: to grow us into a fuller awareness of our true nature.

We're always having the experience that we need to have. How do we know? Because it's happening.

We can reject what comes our way, or we can welcome it. Of course, we're going to get slammed and caught off guard, and we might think, *I do not deserve this. Why me? Source can't be serious.* Feel it all. Wallow if you have to. But don't let those thoughts consume you.

Accepting things as they are is the decision to grow instead of staying stuck. We choose to expand rather than contract. We perceive all events— the welcomed and the unwelcomed—to be a form of healing. The shift into or out of a relationship, the new chapter, the physical challenge or miracle, the upheaval, or the period of peace. It's all for our expansion.

Accepting that everything we experience is for our growth moves us from feeling punished or cast out, toward a sense of being on Team Higher Guidance—with access to its infinite possibilities.

Accepting *what is* moves us from feeling "done to" by life, to "doing life WITH life." We uplevel from victimhood to empowered partnership. We're not in hiding. We get on the dance floor, and we move with the rhythm of the situation. It may feel confusing and frustrating. Some days, life is a mosh pit. Other times, we flamenco.

When we decide not to go rigid and resentful through the dance of life, then life energy will animate our next best move.

Life is not happening to us, it's happening for us. And even more empowering to realize is that it's happening *through* us.

Acceptance Is Dynamic

"Get out of your own way" is a great New Ageism. "Get out of your own way and let it happen." "Once I got out of my own way, it all came together." Once I got out of my own way, I finally got what this means.

True Acceptance Loves the *is-ness* of life. What gets in the way of being able to flow with the is-ness is . . . the small self. The ego identity is always trying to make meaning out of things, like trying to figure out what someone meant by what they said. The small self is constantly trying to maintain its reputation for being in control. Which is crazy because life is inconceivably massive and dynamic.

You "get out of your own way" when you stop trying to control what's happening. You stop using your opinions like they're protective equipment, always defending your choices to other people. You lay off making so many conclusions.

You let your small self sit in the middle of the canoe and let your Higher Self paddle. You get out of the way so you can accept the Love and healing that is always flowing in your direction.

Acceptance Changes Everything

Nothing changes until you accept it.

And to accept it is to Love it *as is*.

That's the vibration of Unconditional Love.

What's your experience when someone Loves you in your less-than-composed moments? You call them bawling your eyes out. When it's supposed to be your best moment and you say the worst thing. Stress made you more aggressive than you know is good for anyone, and you lashed out a bit, or a lot. And your partner, or amazing friend, or a stranger in the ER just looks at you with total calm okayness. They do not even register shock on their face. And they just Love the shit out of you. They might hold you and nod as you spill it all out. They say something simple and assuring.

And you're aware that you are being Loved in your unravelling or shadow spillage. And after you exhale the confusion, you inhale new possibilities. The Love you were shown bridged you from contracted to expanded, and now you can consider making the change that needs to be made. You experienced the Light of Acceptance.

That phenomenon of Acceptance between two people also works between you and the events of your life. Your life acts up. It lashes out. It was supposed to be the best day, and it was a contender for the worst. And you look at your life with total calm okayness, and you just Love the shit out of it. You become the Light of Acceptance.

Accept whatever is happening. It's happening. Let it in. Look it in the eye. Give it a hug. Ask it some questions. And THEN . . . then you and whatever is going on can figure out what to do next—together. This is what it is to be in a Loving relationship with your life.

We expand our consciousness when we accept what's happening. We grow. Resistance is contraction. Acceptance is expansion. Acceptance isn't weakness and passivity. Acceptance is actually highly dynamic because it's in unison with how life is flowing. Are you going to flow in the direction of the drama and fabrication? Or are you going to flow with LIFE? Get on the life cruise—it's always going where you need to be.

Expanding our perspective takes practice. We expand, we conflate. We stretch, we collapse. We extend, we retreat. We believe, we doubt. Einstein reminded us that the Universe is always expanding—and that includes us. Everything is progress—even the apparent detours.

If everything is progress, then there can't be any mistakes. Even mistakes expand us, so . . . you can't get it wrong. "Backwards" might look forward if you see it through a holographic perspective. Think of it this way: accepting our mistakes neutralizes some of the effects of what looks like it was a mistake. And besides, we each have infinity to get everything in order.

Accepting the Unacceptable

Refraining from jumping to conclusions is a sure way to raise your consciousness.

Acceptance doesn't mean that you're condoning what's happening. It means that you're present enough to see what's going on, and you can create some relaxation around the event. And what happens when we relax? We think more clearly.

Acceptance pulls you out of shock and denial. Accepting the difficulties of our times doesn't mean that we'll be infiltrated by the darkness inherent in them. Acceptance helps mitigate overwhelm because it frees up energy to deal with the situation rather than leaking it out to overwhelm or denial.

I was walking around my local lake telling a friend what I'd learned about child trafficking in our own neighborhood. The details were horrific. "I can't believe that's happening. I can't let that into my heart," he said. "I know, it's crushing. But it *is* happening, and if people don't let it land in their awareness, then we won't be able to change it." Denial is a numbing agent that disempowers us. No matter how heartbreaking, the heart will always choose Truth.

Eyes wide open, Love.

In order to accept something—from an inconvenient truth, or a diagnosis, to the post-breakup unknown, **you don't need to know *how* you're going to solve the problem. But facing it with an open mind is how we navigate with presence.**

We can accept what's happening without giving our power over to it. You're scared. Okay. You're doubtful. It's all right. Instead of pushing the fear into the basement, be with it. It won't take you under, it will *wisen and soften you.*

This is an eyes-wide-open approach to the holy human way of being, to the condition and to the gift. There's suffering. I acknowledge it, I can honor it, and I can make choices that will end the suffering.

Resistance Dancing with Willingness

Melanie, one of our Heart Centered Leaders, learned that she had stage 4 cancer. It takes a gorgeous grace to accept a potentially terminal illness. "I know what my body and Soul need to heal, but my anger at the disease in my body turns me to rebellion and choices that don't support me." Some resistance is so holy. The rebellion is such a beautiful part of us. It's how the Spirit raises its fist to life. How our cells confer to bring the body back to balance. How we rally as neighbors and nations to rescue our children and restore our democracies.

Acceptance and resistance are dance partners. Don't stop the dance. You're going to resist transformation. And that can be a good sign. Resistance to change is an indicator that change could be happening. Pushback is a signal that life force might be having an effect on us.

Accept even your resistance. It doesn't need a stern talking to. It needs to be folded into your vision of wellness and fulfillment. If we send our shadow self the message that we're plowing ahead with new protocols for betterment and that it's going to get left in the dust, then the shadow is going to whip up some fear or pain. Naturally. It doesn't want to be left behind.

Evolution includes and then transcends the past. We don't need to get rid of unwanted parts of ourselves, it's all excellent compost for what we're growing.

Everything in the Universe comes from the same Source, indivisible and existing simultaneously. We can't actually "get rid" of anything—but we can transform it. We can also avoid it. We can act like it's not there. We can refuse to take it in. We can try to blow it off. Like, "Bye, debilitation. See you, insecurity. Good riddance, 20 pounds and inflammation."

But the energy of rejection only suppresses the underlying cause of all that's been manifested. You can lose the 20 pounds by shouting hate speech to your body while you work out and limit calories, and you can be really really, happy when you get the physical results you wanted. And all sorts of insights and growth can accompany that physical transformation. But where do the rejected "old" energies and issues go? Nowhere. They're still sitting in the basement of your psyche waiting to be freed up and healed.

Most challenges don't actually go away—just like bad bacteria doesn't suddenly disappear from our bodies. Challenges and bacteria get integrated into our whole system. Embraced, subsumed, made good fodder of.

Trying to dump your "old" self just makes that self-grip harder. What we're trying to get rid of is usually the exact part of ourselves that needs more Love. You can bring it along to your new future. No fragmented self left behind.

We transform our relationship with the challenges, and the challenges themselves will transform. We bring all the parts forward with us. The old is not left behind, it's integrated into our heart and fuels the rise of our energy frequency. That's how real change happens.

Willingness

Just be willing to accept what is, my Love. You don't need to be feeling saintly or stainless. And you may not be completely judgment-free. Just be *willing* to accept, and you've opened the door to higher consciousness.

Willing to open up, to find out. Willing to let go. Willing to Love more today than you did yesterday.

Willingness is a clarion call to your seen and unseen support systems to bring you some aid. The answer you haven't known yet will start to emerge. You will experience revelations that create softness and flexibility within you. You will be met with more . . . Acceptance.

If you were
to look at yourself
with a Loving gaze,
what would shift?

Everything.

Chapter 13

ACCEPTING OTHERS

Receptivity + Discernment = Acceptance

SHE HAS A TENDENCY TO PANIC. Makes it hard to trust her.

They're chronically greedy. Grew up dirt poor. Money is everything.

She is a channel of pure Wisdom, a naturally gifted seer.

He's a genius, able to connect broad intellectual concepts.

He is angry, perpetually antagonistic—much healing to do.

She's just learning to understand the concept of cause and effect.

They find the beauty in everything.

●

People are where they are, despite our desire for them to be further along, more evolved, more fun, closer to our level, less intimidating, more relatable, easier to access, or just more like us.

If you take the desire for someone to be different out of the equation, then you can meet them where they are—and that's how to be Loving. We Love now, we Love as is. This is the essence of dynamic relating, of intimacy. You can connect with each other in the moment and then let your interaction direct the next step.

Acceptance Creates Intimacy

Suspend the wish for someone to be different than they are—that desire is what wedges people apart. If you can stand in front of someone and accept them and their behavior, you're going to have personal access to more life energy, more mental clarity.

Receptivity plus discernment equals Acceptance. The heart accepts, the ego rejects. To see someone as they are, versus how we want them to be, is the virtue of Acceptance. And Acceptance is the sister of discernment.

Accepting someone and their behavior doesn't mean that you're condoning the harmful stuff. It means that you're choosing to operate outside of delusion and manipulation. Accepting the situation or person doesn't mean that we put ourselves in harm's way or expose ourselves to abuse. Acceptance of the situation is to see it very clearly, free of projections, and then from that inclusive vantage point, we can determine if there are any changes that are needed. It means that we seek to understand, and from that open-mindedness, we see better solutions for a better way. Acceptance puts you on solid ground.

"On the surface, acceptance looks like a passive state, but in reality
it is active and creative because it brings something entirely
new into the world. That peace, that subtle energy vibration, is
consciousness, and one of the ways in which it enters this world is
through surrendered action, one aspect of which is acceptance."

–Eckhart Tolle

Krishnamurti taught, "If you begin to understand what you are without trying to change it, then what you are undergoes transformation." This applies to understanding all humans. In a state of Acceptance, we're not wasting energy on retaliation or trying to prove superiority or inferiority. Think of all the energy we could conserve by not trying to assert who's right or wrong. That's a lot of hot air put to better use.

Rejection is a refusal to see or to know things more deeply. **Acceptance is Love in motion.**

Truth exists beyond polarity. Love exists beyond our differences. **If we're in extreme opposition and disagreement, then we haven't found the Truth yet.** Extreme polarization leaves no room for real Acceptance. We can see this playing out across the world.

Acceptance Brings Us into a State of Relaxation

Think about any situation that you're having a tough time accepting right now. How great would it be to just be at peace with it? Again, it doesn't mean you're supporting the situation to continue, you're just here with it today, accepting it as is. Anyone feel relieved?

Acceptance closely relates to the energy of the Divine Feminine that embraces and Loves all of creation. Inclusiveness is our natural state, so being accepting puts our nervous system at ease. Logic might fight it, but the heart settles down our doubts and divisions.

Acceptance Architects Our Boundaries

Creating clear boundaries is an important part in our development. We have to go through the process of realizing "I'm a people pleaser, that's not healthy. I need to have standards and state them and uphold them." That's honoring yourself; that's maturity and self-respect. Fantastic! Now you know what I suggest? Now that you have boundaries, dissolve a lot of them.

We've been conditioned to believe that holding strict boundaries is "better" than accepting a person or the situation as it is.

Healthy boundaries are . . . healthy. But boundaries aren't the end result of divine empowerment. Boundaries are a developmental stage. In some ways, boundaries are a rite of passage to self-awareness. Waking up to the necessity for standards of interaction is part of waking up to your innate worth.

Yet sometimes those structures can become dividing walls. The ego personality loves to build up an arsenal of boundaries, all the reasons things don't work for us. Excessively high standards. Ways we "must" be spoken to and related with. Insistences.

So many of us are wanting to be Loved unconditionally, while we're holding on to a lot of our own conditions. That creates inner conflict. We receive what we give. If we're excessively boundaried, we swing back and forth from a "this works for me" and "this doesn't work for me" pendulum of judgment.

I'm really clear about what works for me and what doesn't. I like to hang out with kind people, I want good food prepared with Love, and I'm a hard pass for heavy metal music in cafés. Except that much of the world is shallow, dirty, and really loud, so if I'm put out when things aren't just so, I'm not doing myself or anyone else any favors—I'm just becoming unbearable with what I don't like to bear.

So . . . boundaries as a developmental part of our awakening? YES. Excessive barriers that divide us into superior and inferior? No need for that.

**Too many rules of engagement get heavy to hold up.
Constriction, resistance, and over-boundedness can be
exhausting. Because those states are not our True Nature.
When we exert so much energy going against our sacred grain,
we get weary. The heart will always choose to find Acceptance.**

I was going for a walk with someone whom I Love and am committed to being a support to. They excel at passive aggression. And I can be excellent at getting offended. You can see where this is going.

The sun was out, dogs were frolicking. My walk partner was not in their best frame of mind, and they threw me a few subtle jabs about my personality. I inwardly rolled my eyes and thought, *Here we go, uh-gain.*

Miraculously, instead of pouncing, I paused. I turned my face to the sun and breathed very, very intentionally into my heart center. And then I told myself the most Buddha-like thing I could think of: *I've got space for them to treat me like shit today. Like, whatever.*

And I meant it. It was a quantum leap. It was the shadow work and all the meditation paying off.

They threw me some more passive-aggressive shade. I let them rant a bit. I accepted them as they were in that moment. I stayed focused on breathing into my heart chakra. I kept looking at the sky.

And then I had an insight: they were in pain (for years) and had no idea how to manage it.

And isn't that part of the human condition? That we're all in some degree of pain and we're just figuring out how to manage it. Until we heal our emotional pain, we're mostly acting out.

In those exchanges where we get emotionally dumped on (and we've all been on both sides—the dumper and the dumpee), can we see someone's Soul behind their behavior? Accept their whole package? And can we also accept our struggle with Acceptance? When we manage to do that, Love flows in, and we remember that we want what's best for that person.

And what's best for all of us most of the time is to be accepted for where we're at.

When I got back home from the walk, my kid asked me how the visit went. And I said, "Kinda great, actually. I just decided to be okay with their total shittiness to me, and it was like, waaay different and easy. And whatever. I am Love and just . . . whatever." I shrugged.

"Ya. 'Whatever' works," he said. Sure does.

PRACTICE
Love Remembers

This is a basic heart centering practice to generate Love between you and someone else—even if you're feeling distant or in opposition to them.

Here it is: Remember why you Love them. So simple. You're going to reach for memories that bring you back together. Tap into the Love you've felt before and bring it into the now.

Recall your best times with someone. You fell in Love for a reason—what was that? Think of your best laughs. Remember how you went out of your way to show them that you Love them, and remember how they showed up for you.

Unblock the Love through intentional recollection. Let your heart soften beyond choices, politics, attitudes—even beyond being judged. And let each other be Loved no matter what. Love flows. Love melts all obstacles. Love unifies. Love remembers us.

Whatever is arising

is coming up

to be healed.

Engage peacefully

with all of it.

Chapter 14

YOUR HEART INTELLIGENCE

Heart centering isn't a poetic concept.
It's a practical practice of physics and spirit.

The Heart Brain

"According to the wisdom traditions of the West (Christian, Jewish,
Islamic) the heart is first and foremost an organ of spiritual perception."
  –Cynthia Bourgeault

It was commonly thought that the brain pulled the levers for all bodily
functions—and it does. But there's a wizard that's highly influencing *the
brain itself*—and it's the heart. Science-driven research is verifying that the
energy and operation of the heart informs the brain and most of our major
organs, as well as our hormonal and nervous systems. The human heart
is an information-processing center with its own functional "brain," now
more commonly referred to as the "heart brain."

(When I hear about science catching up with spirituality, I always envision a bunch of monks doing the slow clap. "Finally getting that the heart
chakra is the engine, eh? K . . . we'll be over here levitating and performing
healing miracles.")

The physical heart and brain are like a driver and car, in constant communication about where the vehicle needs to go. If you want to get somewhere amazing—and *most efficiently*—engage the heart first and then the brain. This is incredibly practical. Using your whole heart, just *intend* to think with Love, or generosity, or goodness, and give that intention over to your thoughts to be operationalized. Here's the strategy: start with Love.

When we let our spirit direct matter, we create something meaningful.

The landmark neurocardiology research of J. Andrew Armour, MD, PhD, in 1991, first established the "heart brain" concept, demonstrating the existence of the heart's own intrinsic nervous system. The heart is by far the strongest source of electromagnetic energy in the body. As peer-reviewed studies have since confirmed, the heart uses that energy to communicate with the brain through four modalities:

neurologically, through the nervous system

biochemically, through hormones and neurotransmitters

biophysically, through pressure waves (heart beats)

energetically, through electromagnetic field interactions (that can extend and be measured several feet away from the body)

Of all the messages sent between the heart and the brain, 90 percent of those are sent from the heart TO the brain. Only 10 percent of this communication starts in the head, the rest of it starts with the heart.

Our intelligent heart. It runs the show.

From the HeartMath Institute:

- In fetal development, the heart forms and starts beating before the brain begins to develop.

- Negative emotions can create a nervous system chaos, positive emotions do the opposite.

- You can boost your immune system by focusing on positive emotions.

According to The HeartMath Institute's 2015 *Science of the Heart*, Volume 2, research overview:

> "**The heart is the most powerful source of electro-magnetic energy in the human body,** producing the largest rhythmic electromagnetic field of any of the body's organs. The heart's electrical field is about **60 times greater** in amplitude than the electrical activity generated by **the brain**. This field, measured in the form of an electrocardiogram (ECG), can be detected anywhere on the surface of the body. Furthermore, **the magnetic field produced by the heart is more than 100 times greater in strength than the field generated by the brain and can be detected up to 3 feet away from the body, in all directions.**"

The Doorway to Your Soul

Most Eastern mysticism regards the heart center to be the seat of the Soul—the center of consciousness in humans. And so it's believed that the best place to concentrate during meditation is the heart chakra.

"The heart chakra (typically 2 to 6 inches in circumference on the body) is a vortex that allows us entry into Higher consciousness—the space beyond polarity, of all expansive inclusiveness. This space is vaster than the sky, with no beginning or end. **We work with the heart chakra so as to identify as the Soul. We're working with the concept of our infinite nature.**

We're not trying to envision everything 'fitting into' the heart vortex. Our awareness is much more expanded. When you work with the heart chakra, you're experiencing the inclusive nature of the heart."

–V.S.

According to most sacred energy practices, our bodies contain a series of energy centers—chakras, that run from the base of the spine to the crown of the head. They go like so:

7th chakra: The Crown, Sahasrara, Radiance

6th chakra: The Third Eye, Ajna, Wisdom

5th chakra: The Throat, Vishuddha, For Giving

4th chakra: The Heart, Anahata, Divine Love, Inclusiveness

3rd chakra: The Solar Plexus, Manipura, Compassion

2nd chakra: The Sacral, Svadhisthana, Loving Kindness

1st chakra: The Root, Muladhara, Resilience

Anahata translates to "unstruck" or "unbeaten." With three chakras below it and three above, the heart chakra is the fulcrum of the body. The heart is the center of it all.

"The heart chakra is the level where one begins to accept and Love everyone and everything unconditionally. One begins to perceive that though people and objects may have gross aspects and differences, they are really embodiments of perfection. One begins to Love people and the objects of the world for what they are. One begins to accept their nature with its faults and positive qualities and to realize that everyone and everything is acting according to its swadharma [that action which is in accordance with your nature]."

–Swami Satyananda Saraswati

Heart Centering

The heart chakra is the portal to Divine Love and all other virtues. It's the gateway to your Higher Self. I can't overstate the magnificence of this. **The heart chakra is a *doorway* within your physical body that leads to higher realms of consciousness.** Knock knock. *Who's there?* INFINITY!

So often we're looking for the shortcut to calmness or the sign about what to do. And we're looking outside of ourselves to authorities, meds, and methodologies. We want to get out of pain and separateness and into something more clarified and stabilized—which, by the way, is an evolutionary impulse. Go directly to the heart.

The heart chakra is like the Narnia wardrobe that leads to an expanded vista, and it's inbuilt in our body.

Your heart is a portal to bliss. Knock with your mind, turn the key with your breath.

Heart centering isn't a poetic concept. It's a practical practice of physics and spirit. It's a metaphysical exercise that increases our vitality.

Here are some heart-related questions for you to ponder. They are beautifully abstract. Maybe you can answer these immediately, free-flow style with your eyes closed. If not, you can get back to me:

How does your heart center feel as you become more heart centered?

What does it actually feel like to have an expanded awareness of the power of your heart chakra?

What's the metaphysical experience of being more Loving?

●

It seems to be a common experience that as we become more present to Love, we experience both a sense of fullness and emptiness. It's almost indescribable. Our heart center feels full of space. It's overflowing with vastness.

Think of a person or pet that you Love deeply. Alive or passed on. Or sit in your Love for Mother Nature or God Force Itself. Close your eyes and breathe in the awareness of that Loving. Can you feel that cool-warm, open fullness? And do you notice how it feels like it's coming from behind your heart? It might be as if the "spirit" of Love is standing right behind you, gently supporting you to face forward.

The consciousness that is Divine Love informs matter and bends time. This is what it feels like to focus our attention on it. Direct your attention into your heart and let that energy guide your thoughts, words, and actions.

How do we raise the frequency of Love in our being, in our lives, in the world?

Simply focus your attention on your heart center.

THOUGHTS + FEELINGS

Chapter 15

DESIRE HIGHER

Let go and see what remains.

Desirelessness?

According to some Buddhist principles, the spiritual aim is to exist in a state of desirelessness. The aim is to be so unified with the Infinite that we want for nothing, unfolding only with the perpetual now.

When you realize that the Universe exists within you, what's more to want?

To desire desirelessness, well . . . you can see the irony. Eventually, even the aim for enlightenment has to fall away in this case. What we're likely left with is an open-handed offering to life. Giving and receiving. Aware that the divine will of heaven is also our will. *"Thy will be done, on Earth as it is in heaven."*

Desire is part of the full human experience. If you have a thinking mind, desirelessness will be impossible. I've had this conversation with Buddhist lamas, rabbis, and Unity ministers. And we all agree that the spiritual aim is not necessarily about being desireless.

"Is it possible to be desireless? No. Actually it is not possible. As long as the mind is there, its duty is to desire . . . the secret is that any desire without any personal or selfish motive will never bind you."

–translated by Sri Swami Satchitananda

We will desire, that's that. But perhaps we should try to desire higher, for more inclusive and healing experiences.

So higher desire is not about "aiming" at the target of what you want and not stopping 'til you get it. A heart centered approach to desire is about being open to your Soul's guidance of what's best for you—and for all beings. So desire becomes much less motivational—"Do exactly this to get exactly that"—and entirely aspirational: *Thy will be done, on Earth as it is in heaven.*

Our fulfillment is predicated on the content of our desires. Higher desire is a focus on higher-vibration states of being— virtues of the heart—rather than worldly getting. Our focus includes the benefit of all beings, and we go about our manifesting with fierce gentleness. There's no grasping. Just a deep dedication to Loving Kindness.

Let Go and See What Remains

Humanity is going through a monumental passage of change—a prophe-sied Golden Age that's kicking off with an extended detox. The collective shadow is surfacing to be healed. It's narrow and harrowing, exhilarating and expanding. Every one of us has a load to bear and gifts to bring to the transformation of the planet.

Each of us will have to consider throwing things overboard to make it over the rapids of upheaval and regeneration. It's *heave-ho!* time for the opinions, grievances, materialism, and self-centered ambitions that are no longer appropriate in a world in need of group Love and determination.

For my part in the planetary tribulation and unfolding, I thought it'd be a great time to have an existential crisis and a yard sale. I began with considering my mortality and assessing my eco-unfriendly habits. Giving up pedicures and dyeing my hair wasn't a hardship. But then I had to contemplate the stuff with more gravitas.

I became obsessed with considering my death. **What would I have to do to prepare to die, free and clear?** There were people I had to Forgive—and ask Forgiveness of. There were some Love letters to write. I wanted to give away some possessions that friends admired. *I'm going to die someday, might be 40 years from now, but I know you always wanted this sweater, so just have it.*

(It's worth noting that as I prepared to live freer and die with a cleaner conscience, in no way did I feel compelled to lose more weight, work longer hours, or go shopping.)

Okay. *Thy will be done.* Let's go there . . .

I reviewed the three strongest desires of my existence: to stay alive, to keep doing meaningful work, to create a life with a great partner.

And after a lot of contemplation and consideration, one Saturday afternoon after some furious and prayerful dancing to Florence and the Machine, I worked up the courage to tell God that I was (finally) handing it all upward. On my knees, planted in shag carpet, heart pounding, the conversation went something like this:

"I know we're shifting from a 'My will be done' to a 'THY will be done' business model. I got it. I'm quite terrified because, as you know, I have a deep-seated fear that your will is to punish me (Catholic hangover). I'm working that out. That's my responsibility.

"Here goes. I'm giving my desires over to you. Take my life if you need it. If I'm meant to die in the near future, then so be it. If my son's path is to lose me, then I'll support him from the other side. *Thy will be done.*

"Take my career. If you think it's best for me to walk away from my profession, I'm willing to radically simplify. I can disappear and get by. Social media's a circus anyway. *Thy will be done.*

"If it's my calling to be an urban monk without a romantic partner, then, okay. I can source my joy solo. I'm up for it. *Thy will be done.*

"Lord, make me an instrument of your peace. Where there is hatred, let me sow Love."

And I offered it all up that day, as truly and thoroughly as I possibly could. And I felt . . . *so relieved.* Not terrified like I thought I should. Just calm. I reconciled the possibility of dying and the fact that that could leave my teenage son devastated and rudderless. And I still left it up to God, knowing that we all, even my son, have our path and sorrow that remakes us into devotees of life.

If my business needed to tank, fine, whatever. I'm resourceful. I subsisted on ramen noodles for most of my twenties; I'm sure I could do it again.

And after years of pining for "my king," I surrendered to how truly solid I was on my own, with so many sources of Love flowing into my life. What a relief that I wasn't going to be scouting for The One in every airport and cafe. "Could that be him?" I could just put my hair up in a topknot and *relax.*

I cleaned up some of my affairs. I had some exquisite conversations. I deleted my dating apps. And I rolled around in the new spaciousness of my life. Truly, I'd let it all go. The relief was really amazing and invigorating.

And . . . then . . . over that year . . . the same desires grew back. I could not deny them. But this time they felt more like flowers than weeds.

So I got back on my knees one Saturday afternoon and spoke from the center of my heart—the home base of courage. And I laid it out for the Infinite: *I trust my humanity and my holiness. Can we please work together on life, Love, and happiness?*

I decided that I wanted to live—more than ever, actually. The lite plaguing feeling I had for most of my life of wanting to get off this Babylon ride and port back to my star home . . . it evaporated. Whatever is unfolding on the planet, I'm up for it.

Every sign pointed to staying the course with my vocation. Why would I not do what life built me to do? So I got to writing this book.

And as for the man partner . . . well, you know how that story was going to go. I reinstalled one dating app, and brunch the following weekend turned out to be the Love of my life.

My desires returned, but the associations around them had shifted. In my sincere letting go of what I wanted, the striving energy dislodged. And what was left was . . . just what I wanted.

What desires free you?

How can your fulfillment benefit others?

Are you willing to let go of desires to see what lives in your heart center?

Goal Setting and Forgetting

I don't have much to say about goals other than that . . . they're ridiculous.

I'm laughing when I say that, but I'm not even kidding.

Let me unpack that. Let's start with the state of the world.

How do you set goals when the world's falling apart? Well . . . why bother? I mean, the world. is. falling. apart. (Which is a necessary and good thing.) But given that's the case, who cares if we hit our Q2 objectives or lose 10 pounds by the new year?

I've been writing about goal setting for years, in a perpetual swing of resistance and flow with the topic. And I've officially come to the conclusion: goals aren't all that.

I've set goals. Massive and micro goals. I've hit the goals, exceeded some of them, and failed at plenty. For me, reaching or missing goals did not make me a more enlightened or Loving person. More experienced? Yes. More stressed out? Definitely. More self-critical? For sure.

The fact is that I'm going to do my best no matter what, and some days, my best is awesome, and some days, my best blows. But my best is what I'm giving on any given day because I'm a human doing her best. Sometimes it's really hard to do my best, and sometimes best is like butter.

I have discovered that I'm at my best without the goals.

And what's more . . . what will be, will be, whether I set a benchmark or not. The Divine Plan does not require metrics or motivational incentives to unfold.

Here's the thing . . . **motivational routines place the power outside of yourself**—even if you're the one setting the goals. If you hit it, you're a winner. If you miss it, you're a . . . misser. This isn't liberation. This is a reward and punishment system.

Goals can be fun and useful, for sure. Ga'head, have goals. Juicy ones, even. Cash flow projections are smart business. Racing your personal best is extremely satisfying. But it's all just data. And you are not your data—or your achievements. And life is not a race.

If we set goals, we need to be very mindful about the driving force behind them. Because, as I've been saying for years, "do or die" goals can kill your spirit.

But! There is a useful tactic for both chronic goal setters as well as those of us just goin' with the flow. This works if you need to light a fire under your ass, or if your heart is fully ablaze: VISION.

Aspiration—or vision—is a very different kind of energy than what goal setting brings. Vision springs from within your heart. You aspire because your heart, not your head, is directing you. Goals can be a slippery ego-slope. The intellect Loves its measurables and the ego Loves its pride. But the heart sees through all of that.

"Where there is no vision, the people perish."
–Proverbs 29:18

So let's talk about VISION. Having a vision is essential to creating. Vision is how we stay on the path to Love. Vision is the difference between falling for old social programming and fashioning a life from the Light of your Soul.

Aspiration looks upward to Source for its cues. It might go like this:

Dear Infinity, I am devoted. I'm here to serve, I am not without fear, I am not without blind spots, but I'm earnest, and I'm willing. Light the way.

Or this more-to-the-point prayer:

Hello, Soul. Show me what to want.

PRACTICE
May All Be So Blessed

One of the simplest, most powerful prayers we can say is "May all be so blessed."

What are you grateful for? Can you wish for everyone to have that same reason to be grateful?

Name your blessing or gratitude and wish it upon all beings. It's a powerful micro-practice to bring with you everywhere: *May all be so blessed.*

Thank you for this meal. May it nourish me. *May all be so blessed.*

I'm so thankful for reliable transportation. *May all be so blessed.*

I'm better than ever. *May all be so blessed.*

I'm so grateful for clean drinking water. *May all be so blessed.*

Vitamins, thank you for supporting me. *May all be so blessed.*

I made a full recovery. *May all be so blessed.*

We're so deeply in Love. *May all be so blessed.*

We're safe and sound. *May all be so blessed.*

This sunlight, this walk. *May all be so blessed.*

Money to pay my expenses. *May all be so blessed.*

These hugs that heal me. *May all be so blessed.*

Food from the garden. *May all be so blessed.*

I have it so good in so many ways. *May all be so blessed.*

May all be so blessed.

Lighten your load

and you'll see

what matters most.

Work less to buy stuff

to impress people that

haven't yet considered

Loving you unconditionally.

Live lightly on

the land that keeps us alive.

Simplify to deepen.

Chapter 16

THOUGHTS ON FEELINGS

What can our emotions be in service of?

REFLECTION. Let's do a feeling experiment. We'll use sadness as the sample test. Think about a sad feeling that you've had in the past or that you're currently experiencing. Observe yourself feeling the sadness.

How do you know that you're sad? How do you know that what you're feeling should be called "sadness"? What else is that sadness attached to? Is this sadness connected to prior events with the same vibration, texture, or association?

When and how did you learn to be sad? Did someone model sadness for you? Did they let you know what should make you sad and, by default, what should make you happy?

Take a few breaths and let that sadness drift out the nearest window.

Now let's ponder anger for a minute.

Suppose that a friend was supposed to pick you up at a certain time to drive you to the train station. And they were late, and so you missed the last train home. You were really disappointed about missing the train, and you felt angry toward them.

What made you think that you should have an angry reaction specifically toward them? Was it a build-up of their previous behavior that triggered your anger? Were you ever told a long time ago by family or teachers that late people are disappointing? Did you witness someone in your household, school, or in a movie being reprimanded for being late?

How did you learn to be angry?

Okay, let the imaginary anger go. Take a deep, cleansing breath.

We acquire a lot of our feelings from past experiences and social conditioning. We collect those past experiences like color swatches and pull them out to match our experience in the present time. "This is happening, and therefore, pleasure, sadness, anger, regret, excitement is the fitting response." We roll out the gloomy response when the weather isn't what we want it to be. We crank up the excitement when we think we're getting the gift we want. *This is happening, or I assume this will happen in the immediate future; therefore, I should feel . . .*

Emotions are habitualized thoughts. And by their very nature, habits are reactive—you don't have to consciously think about doing the action or repeating the thought, whether it's reaching for your phone, saying "Excuse me" when you bump someone, or reacting when people cut you off in traffic.

If many of our emotions are habitual, then how do we be genuinely present in all situations? How can we create a **flowing alertness** so we meet each person and event with what that moment needs from us?

It might help to understand that **emotions come from the past**. Every emotion has a reference point that's connected to something that happened or something we were taught or trained to believe before this current moment. Emotions live in the subconscious. They hang out in the shadow zone.

Emotions are watery in nature. Emotions are experienced from the lower chakras in our physical body.

Emotions don't emerge from the heart center. The heart is the *portal to consciousness*, not a receptacle of the unconscious. The heart is wakeful, not reactive. The heart transmits virtues—which are higher states of consciousness.

Even though emotions can pendulum between pleasure and pain, emotions aren't "bad" or base, they're just a part of our whole makeup. Storm clouds, fluffy clouds . . . all a part of nature.

Emotions are a fantastic, beautiful, messy, glorious part of being human. They are the instinctiveness that saves our lives, that have us pursue our passions and callings. Emotions are the flavor of our humanity. Emotions can help us employ our free will.

Every single feeling arises to be experienced and integrated into our hearts. Which is to say, every emotion is trying to get our attention. Our attention, our mindfulness, is one of the currencies of our Love.

When we ignore our emotions, they become more persistent or intensified over time. Neglecting or partitioning off our emotions doesn't actually free up our energy to do the other things we'd much rather be doing. Like, "I shall will myself not to feel my sadness, or the jealously, or to surrender to the ecstasy . . . so that I can be more productive, supportive, or balanced." It doesn't work that way.

Feelings are a form of energy. And even the so-called negative or dark feelings come bearing potential dynamism and Light. If we don't truthfully acknowledge how we're feeling, we create energy blockages. Worse than that, we miss out on the expansiveness that comes from being conscious and attentive to our interior experience. Neglected feelings are missed insights.

I'll give you this highly enlightened perspective of mine: I was ashamed that I was resenting a friend for being such a drag. I was feeling super unspiritual about it all. So I didn't admit to myself that I was resentful. But man, it was getting rough putting up with their melancholy. But because I wanted to be an endlessly patient, yogic, and evolved friend, I "acted" endlessly patient to . . . myself.

Extending patience to another person is an act of Love and selflessness. Telling yourself that you only ever feel light about the heavy lifting of Love is just self-deception. Lying to yourself is a setback.

So I had a confessional talk with myself while loading the dishwasher one night. You know the kind, domesticity as introspection. And without any rancor toward my suffering friend, because my heart is so truly in Love with them, I turned my patience to myself and admitted, *This no-fun shit is wearing me the shit down.* And I felt a surge of relief, happiness, and Love.

And that wave of energy helped me resolve to keep Loving them through what they needed to be Loved through. And . . . I booked a hotel that weekend to give myself a break. Win-win.

●

When we over-privilege some emotions, they turn into the house guests that never want to leave.

Emotions in and of themselves aren't a problem. What's problematic though is identifying as our emotions and getting pulled off center into their highs and lows. We can let emotions cloud our vision, or we can pull back and see them as weather patterns—and from there, we decide to take shelter or head outside.

There is a more balancing and liberating path, and it travels toward embodying virtues. In this way, we tap in to the divine energy that is beyond thought and feeling, the energy that evolves us. We begin to know that we're not our emotions. We are much more powerful, creative, and eternal.

Emotions are like a global positioning system that signals how close we are to our hearts.

> "Our feelings are only ever pleasant or unpleasant, and never right or
> wrong. This is something Buddhist psychology strongly emphasizes . . .
> You need not be ashamed of any feeling you experience. You feel what you
> feel. Simply accepting this is in itself a profound act of self-compassion."
> –Bodhipaksa

Every emotion is carrying a message for us. The stronger the negative emotion, the closer it is to an unhealed wound. The emotion is trying to get our attention to say, "There's something unhealed over here, and it needs your help." Sometimes we can make an obvious connection between our current emotions and experiences that were impressed upon us from the past. *When he talks to me with that tone, it makes me feel agitated because it reminds me of when my father said similar things to me and I felt discounted.* That awareness might help you relate to the present differently and come into more ease and balance.

But we don't have to connect every real-time emotional flare-up or sensation to an event in our childhood or a past-life trip. Really, there's no need to overthink most of this stuff. That just keeps us in habituated thinking and guilt traps.

"It doesn't matter how things feel. Don't use feelings as a gauge for whether things are right or wrong. There is a clear, silent inner spaciousness that is much more significant to be aware of than mere feelings. Feelings, moods, and thoughts come and go and are perceived. The tendency or habits to identify with them is also perceived. Somehow, the one who perceives is the most overlooked. And this is what I am pointing to over and over again. Although consciousness perceives the momentary, it also has the power to ignore everything. It is ever untouched and unchangingly present. You alone can confirm this to be true."

–Mooji

You can have feelings about your feelings and thoughts about your thoughts, thoughts about your feelings, and feelings about your thoughts. And sometimes we feel other people's feelings. It's all pretty amazing if you really think about it.

●

We do not have to process everything in order to grow.

We can just feel the feeling. And if we so choose, we can assess the effects of that feeling on us, what thoughts accompany it, if it comes with fresh perspectives or ideas, and if the feeling needs more curiosity or respect from us. And we can let it go and experience the next feeling passing through. And hopefully between the feelings, we can rest in the vibrant calm of the heart space—beyond thinking about our feelings having feelings about our thoughts.

We want to witness, honor, and learn from our feelings. We want to interpret the signals that our emotions are always sending us. **We want to fully feel our feelings without over-identifying with them**. Feel them and release them. Love them, don't try to possess them. Like the weather patterns passing through a sheltering sky.

"Keep the windows open, allow thoughts to come and go."

–Zen Master Suzuki

Keep Calm and Get Heart Centered

We've all ridden the emotional roller coaster. It jacks up stress, wears on our self-esteem, and clouds our thinking. Emotionality creates a kind of static electricity in our system that makes it harder for Wisdom and Light to pour into our energy bodies—our thinking (the mental body), our energy currents (the etheric body), and our actual physical body.

Emotional reactivity can turn into a form of (private) entertainment. Even when we claim to want peace, we may be secretly addicted to the thrilling "fun" of stress. But breathe. It's not a spiritual bypass to actively calm your emotions—it's healthy self-governance.

This is the aspiration: to be centered no matter what. We center, we calm, we feel life force breathing and guiding us, and we build spiritual, psychological, and physical strength.

It's urgent that we learn to return to calm—our heart center, equanimity.

Let's spotlight one of the emotions that can be the most destructive when it's left totally unsupervised: anger.

Maybe you've been here: your temper flares, the anger escalates, and you find yourself screaming in your car or shouting into a pillow until your voice is hoarse.

How do you feel after the scream fest? Relieved and high vibe, or . . . empty but dried out? Slightly . . . devastated.

I've screamed in my car, I have pounded the pillows, and I have only felt . . . empty and slightly dried out. And honestly, a bit embarrassed that I lost my shit, even if it was in the privacy of my own freak-out.

I would never suggest that we deny or suppress anger. See it, honor it, let it pass through you. Don't let it tear you up in the process. Anger becomes a weapon when we point it in the wrong direction for the wrong reason. So it's useful to ask if we're raging toward someone else or about our own behavior. Are we pouring rage on top of rage? Are we looking for another fight?

Don't identify with the anger. Your heart is vast . . . the anger is just a storm. You can bring out the sun of your consciousness to help it dissipate.

Alternatively, is our anger a burning sorrow that longs to bring things into balance? A deep impulse to right the wrongs, rather than seek revenge or more destruction?

We lash out when we don't show our own anger Compassion—when we keep it outside of ourselves. When we bring our anger into our heart center, it will diffuse and give us the teaching that it needs to. When we acknowledge the emotion (anger) that we're feeling, we're showing it the respect it's demanding. Then, like a furious defendant who just wants her day in court, we allow the anger to state its case. That's usually all it wants: To be heard. To be accepted. To be seen. And then we can move on.

Fight your anger and it will fight you right back. And before you know it, you could be spinning out of control, making a mess of things. Have Compassion for your anger and you can go so far as to lead others to fair and equitable solutions.

In the inclusive energy of the heart, anger can become a *holy anger*. It's an anger that is felt on behalf of the greater good. It sees the sweeping injustice and rallies for a resolution that will uplift *everyone*. It may burn, but it never lashes out. Holy anger can blaze a path to Compassion.

Thinking Out Loud

It's wise to be mindful of our language around heavy emotions. You are not sadness. You are not anger. You are *feeling* sadness or anger. "I'm sad" is a validation that lets the emotion sink deeper into your psyche. "I'm feeling sad" respects that you're allowing the emotions space to come and go.

•

Embodying Love

A meaningful life isn't necessarily predicated on how we feel. Ultimately, our emotions do not define our degree of service, our spiritual growth, or our satisfaction with our experience on the planet.

Shifting from an emotion-driven life to a more heart centered life is a developmental process. With experience and reflection, our emotional literacy increases. We can sense and name a greater variety of emotions. Instead of broad brushstrokes like, "I was hurt," we can identify the finer hues of disappointment, rejection, or fear of losing control. Happiness variegates into connection, delight, sharingness.

We can be experiencing grief and feel deeply connected to Source. There may be periods of time when happiness is elusive, but we're growing in profound ways. You can feel sad and bring happiness to another person's day. We can steadily evolve within the emotional highs and lows.

Emotions and desire are evolutionarily useful, but they're not what we're evolving toward. If we let emotions and desires run our show, we're in for a lot of drama and distraction.

The higher aim is to put the heart in the lead, honoring our emotions as they arise, and put all of our desires to work for inclusive Love—for everyone's happiness.

For periods of growth, our guiding question will, and should be, *How do I want to feel?* As we're waking up to our creative capacity, that question advances us on the path of self-knowledge. Knowing how it is that you want (and don't want) to feel orients you to your choicefulness. It also helps heighten bodily awareness and read its cues. Your feelings become map markers to what you want to manifest.

How do I want to feel? is an essential inquiry for self-awareness and honoring our humanity.

But we can't stop there.

We keep rising. Including and transcending our experiences. We activate our higher energy centers. We grow *upward*.

And then a new question takes us even further into the heart:

What do I want to embody?

Chapter 17

FEELINGS ABOUT THOUGHTS

We can choose the quality of our thoughts.

WE EXIST, WE THINK, WE FEEL. But . . . we tend to overthink, get consumed by feelings, and forget that we are pure existence.

Thoughts and emotions intertwine. One influences the other. Thoughts can stir up feelings, feelings can direct thoughts. I don't think it matters which comes first, the thought or the feeling. And in terms of our capacity to live from the heart, being a "thinker" or a "feeler" is not more advantageous than the other. We each have our dispositions, and we'll all get to the heart in our own way.

I've tried to empty my mind of thoughts. Didn't work. I still thought about not having thoughts. That's the thing with the mind—it's always thinking about itself. And trying to wrestle with thoughts that we don't want to think can perpetuate more thinking that we don't want. It's exasperating.

CHOCOLATE. Dark chocolate. Milk chocolate. Melt in your mouth chocolate. Now try to not think about chocolate. Stop seeing chocolate in your mind right now. You could say to yourself, "Right now, I will stop thinking about chocolate" (or "I will stop thinking about my ex, or my skin, or my job . . ."). It's futile.

The mind will think. The mind's job is to create thoughts, and those thoughts will likely create some feelings. And then you'll probably have some feelings about the feelings. It's all good. What we need to keep in mind is that . . .

We can choose what to think.

> "The truth is that you are responsible for what you
> think, because it is only at this level that you can exercise
> choice. What you do comes from what you think."
> –*A Course in Miracles*

We can choose the *quality* of our thoughts. We can point our thoughts in a higher direction. We can go to quality resources to inspire quality thinking. Just like fueling our body with nutritious food, we can fuel our mind with nutritious content—ideas, paradigms, images, stories, sounds, textures of Truth, colors of Loving.

Manifestation happens in the mind.

Choosing our thoughts is top priority for a purposeful life (and the future of humanity).

The mind is the most numinous instrument of creation that we have. We feed thoughts and ideas to our mind, and the mind materializes reflections of those thoughts and ideas.

This is tricky terrain when you consider that we have a conscious mind and an *unconscious* mind, that we're multidimensional beings living in a fourth-dimensional reality. There's all the thinking that happens on the upper floor of our house—our consciousness awareness. We can hear what we're telling ourselves, we're cognizant of what's making us feel certain ways. We can "see" our thoughts. And we're intentionally using particular thoughts and ideas to keep us heading in the direction we want to go. We're consciously using our consciousness to create more consciously. It's amazing!

But then we have all kinds of thinking that happens in the basement of our psyche—thoughts in our subconscious. Without further inspection, we have no idea what's going on down there, but whatever it is, it's still under our roof, and it has an effect on our atmosphere.

We increase our chances of a fulfilling existence when we get more intentional about what thoughts, and images, and sounds we are giving to our mind.

What about old messages and memories, positive or negative, that cross our mind and influence our feelings and therefore our behavior? What about the thoughts that slide in and rise without our conscious invitation?

Free will, my Love. We get to choose which thoughts we focus on and which thoughts we refuse. You do not have to believe any life-dampening thoughts. Ever. No matter how long they've been circulating or where they came from. Replace them with more Loving, peaceful thoughts.

So! Since the path to our Buddha Nature involves a lot of human thinking . . . And since it's metaphysical law that ENERGY FOLLOWS THOUGHT . . . we best use our thoughts to create ease, beauty, and harmony.

Knowing that we direct our energy and healing with our thoughts, let's choose our thoughts with intention.

Wise Thinking

You think it, and you will begin to feel it.

You will *feel the energy of that thought.*

You feel it, and you will begin to believe it.

You believe it, and you will begin to see it.

Choose your thoughts wisely.

> "Before you build any thoughtform, check your thoughts.
> Thoughts originating from beauty, goodness, and truth live
> eternally and ornament space with their symphonic beauty."
> –Torkom Saraydarian

REFLECTION. Take three seconds and create a thought right now about your health. Maybe it's about your immune system, body mass, youthfulness, strength, or overall vitality. What's an opinion or a statement you feel inclined to make about your health?

Got a thought about your health? Okay. Would you call that a positive or negative thought? What's the energy of that thought? Is the thought trusting and beautiful? Is it demeaning or fearful? Is that thought supportive or destructive? Or is it more neutral?

Thoughts are magnetic in nature. The energy of a thought is what that thought will attract. Put a Loving thought into your mind and Loving energy will flow in to meet that thought. Place an encouraging thought into a conversation, and hopeful and optimistic ideas will follow.

REFLECTION. Let's try this in reverse. Let's start with the energy and then create a specific thought.

Choose the energy that you want to emanate: Loving Kindness. Happiness. Generosity. Breathe into your heart and feel that energy already present within you.

What's a thought that encapsulates the energy that you want to emanate?

Now use that heart centered energy to generate thoughts about your health. And your relationships. And the whole wide world.

Use Love to think with.

Conditioning

Introvert. Extrovert. Gemini. Virgo. Catholic. Bohemian. Attached. Single. Responsible. Worthy. Educated. Respectful. Dutiful. Upbeat. Strong. Positive. Cynical. Scientific. Rational. Emotional.

Keep going . . .

Vows. Contracts. Grades. Regulations. Mandates. Clubs. Hierarchy. Personality Tests. Segregation. Caste Systems. Rules of Engagement.

What do these roles and constructs mean? Whatever we make them mean. And the meaning we assign to something depends on what we're identifying as. As dense matter or pure energy, obligated or sovereign. The sky or the weather.

For the longest time, I liked to label myself as an introvert. Loved to wave my introvert flag (not too high though). My introvert membership meant I didn't have to talk to my neighbors much. Drawing the drapes was acceptable behavior. It also meant that I could sit in the corner at a party and talk to one person all night, even if it was to avoid talking to other people that night. I'm not shy. I'm not hemmed in by social anxiety or stage fright, I was just . . . an introvert. The label held me back from my full range of Love and presence.

Some days I'm very, very quiet. Lots of the time, I want to chat it up with strangers. If I check in with my heart first, instead of my persona, then no matter where I am or who I'm with, I'm more available for Love. This approach works for all the concepts and behaviors that I attached myself to over the years: what it means to be in a committed partnership, to be good at business, to be spiritually devoted. I ask my heart what it means every day.

The thing with appearances is that you have to maintain them or people get disappointed with your organic evolution. Self-agency is hard to commodify and restrain. This is how we get stuck in the same job for years—deadening or high octane. This is why we end up having to clean houses full of things we don't use much. It's how tyrannical "leadership" festers. It's why many of us stay in deadening relationships. Because we think we have to keep being what we've always been to get what we want. And that's the ultimate mind conditioning.

●

We all have some story lines about ourselves that we carry around. *I'm an achiever. I work hard. I always do my best. I'm stubborn. I'm not good with women. I can do anything. I create my own reality. I'm physically fragile. I am blessed beyond measure.*

Like emotions, our narratives about ourselves come from the past. Our stories about the past are doing their best to protect us from the perceived dangers of the future. Although the intention seems good (keeping us safe), narratives can wall us off from future (good!) possibilities.

Those stories can also keep us fixated on ensuring our safety. Whether that's with alarm systems, or insurance policies, or constant sanitizing, or protecting ourselves from the heart break of dating apps. Life's inherent unpredictability threatens our constructs of safety. And when it comes to full-on, wide-awake living, some of us are more risk-averse than others. That depends on how we choose to see life.

We can regard the Universe as friendly or hostile. And that depends on the stories we tell ourselves about whether life is conspiring in our favor or not. And life will support our theories in the form of the people who show up for us to open doors or teach us about betrayal.

Ancestry, inheritance, genetics, data, statistics, research, folklore, mythology, legacy. Most stories about the present and future are based on the past. So how do we write a new story as we go forward? We have to recognize that we are a narrative in progress. And we get to write a plot twist anytime. We don't know the ending of our story yet, but it's helpful to assume the best.

In a disconnected world, hope and Faith are leadership qualities.

> "There is no standard for one who is liberated. You neither have to give all your things away nor live naked in some cave. Truth is not like that. Each expression is unique. A liberated being may have a hundred houses, yet they do not pursue wealth. Another is without possessions and with no cares in the world. Both these beings are free and equally happy, not being enslaved by the things of the world."
> –Mooji

●

Since our emotions and thoughts intermingle, similar to being taught how to feel about certain things, much of our thinking is conditioning. "I'm good, bad, fat, thin, rich, poor . . ." This is scripting that someone else (the culture, religion, media, mythology) wrote and started reading to us from inception.

REFLECTION. What's an original thought that you have about yourself? Don't think too hard about that answer. Because none of us has any original thoughts about ourselves or the world around us. Nothing to be ashamed of. We've all been falling for the same dualistic story line for eons. Your parents and their parents and 70 generations back and sideways were all born into the same limiting drama about what's right and wrong, and what should belong to whom, and who should get in to heaven or be granted a low-interest mortgage.

The human drama is just a cluster of thoughts that we agree to keep thinking. We buy into duality and "me versus them" behavior (literally, thanks to capitalism). So how does that dualism influence our individual personality? Well, it means that our personalities are somewhat fabricated.

We instinctively create personas in order to navigate "safely" in the world. Some of us pull from family traits, some of us emulate our heroes. Some of us do what we're told. Some of us play the role of the rebel. Of course we have deeply individual preferences and expressions.

But if we're not our thoughts, then we're not our personalities either. And if you can change your thinking and, in turn, your feelings, then you can also shift your persona. It's called fitting in, surviving, and thriving. Even the rebels do it. But if you try to change your personality to please others, it's only as good as changing your costume. What's underneath the persona remains the same. And that's great news. (What's eternal is always good news.) We are each human expressions of a Higher Soul.

Here's the inside-out approach: If you start to change what you think about who you are at your inner core—what you identify with—then the outer personality will begin to shift. The persona will become more translucent. You'll become less of a self and more of your Self. And that's when inner peace is revealed.

Take. the. Red. Pill.

Day in and day out, most of us consume so much information that we can't hear ourselves think or feel what we're feeling. The endless flow of media is hypnotic, and the nature of much of the content is coding our unconscious mind for disconnection, heartache, and failure.

Lotta "love" songs from all eras are about longing, loss, and first-degree revenge. You're gonna lose, get left, or pine for eternity for someone that never treated you right. And, Lord, I won't even get started on the feast of misogyny and degraded sexuality that is in much mega mainstream music.

Spend four minutes sampling the music charts or news, and every time you hear a message that's mean-spirited, derogatory, victimized or victimizing, sad, depressing, hopeless, flaunting materialism, or in a crippling state of wanting what's bad for anyone's own good . . . just turn it off.

Now do that with every movie. And TV show. And the news. It's going to get really quiet.

Turn on your heart, un-condition your mind.

If the message is to scare you, turn it off. If it tells you that you're not worthy, turn it off. If it's predicting heartbreak, inciting violence on your spirit, or trying to pit you against any other being on the planet, turn it off. If it tells you that your heart will never mend, *Goodbye*. Doesn't matter if it has a great backbeat, or it comes from an elected official or someone claiming to know Saint Someone.

If it doesn't speak, shine, or vibe about the greater good of all, turn it off.

Why does the negative stuff stick into our minds? Why doesn't it bounce off us? The negative messaging will stick in your consciousness because your natural state is peaceful. Your mind is registering an intruder.

Add to that the power of repetition, rhythm, and optics, and we can be dangerously subjectable to the power of suggestion.

We're being influenced all the time. We can choose better influences.

Inside Out

> "Do not conform to the pattern of this world, but
> be transformed by the renewing of your mind."
>   –Romans 12:2

There are all kinds of methodologies and mind habits for making progress in life. Except not every tool that gets you immediate or surface results is helping you to make true progress.

Speed reading is great, as long as you're still able to savor what you've read. We can grow muscle mass, but are we in sync with our body's inherent intelligence? We can extend our life span, but are we living? What good are the shortcuts and optimizations if we're not syncing with the pulse of nature and the laws of the Universe? What's driving our obsession with optimization and human performance measurements? Could be an evolutionary impulse. Could be the ego on steroids.

You can't life hack your way to Wisdom. The heart wants to take us to the revelatory place where we identify as something greater than our body and personalities, to the depth of consciousness where we do not fear death or old age. And further still to where we self-activate the Wisdom in our own cells. There's so much exciting science being unfurled to support our wellness. But the greatest frontier is where the mind meets the Divine.

ENERGY FOLLOWS THOUGHT

ENERGY FOLLOWS THOUGHT

ENERGY FOLLOWS THOUGHT

ENERGY FOLLOWS THOUGHT

ENERGY FOLLOWS THOUGHT

ENERGY FOLLOWS THOUGHT

ENERGY FOLLOWS THOUGHT

ENERGY FOLLOWS THOUGHT

ENERGY FOLLOWS THOUGHT

Chapter 18

LOVING THOUGHTS

**Loving thoughts are the healed edition
of the unloving scripts we've had on repeat.**

WE CAN CHOOSE beauty in chaos. We can choose ease in struggle.

Suffering begins and ends in the mind, so we can use our mind to make higher-vibration choices. To do this, we'll have to heal the habits of the mind—the constant seeking, comparing, and berating.

We can use the energy of our hearts to help the mind relax and open. And we can use the energy of our hearts to guide the mind toward more Loving thoughts.

This requires vigilance. This is the real work of Light work: to observe our thoughts without judgment, and when we notice heavy thoughts passing through, to acknowledge their presence and then create a more Loving thought. Observing the heavy clouds and bringing out the sun.

Our thought cadence might go something like this: Positive thought, positive thought, positive . . . negative thought. Negative thought. Negative, negative, negative. More negative. Big positive thought swoops in. Positive. Negative. Pos-, pos-, positive.

And don't you know it, that process can span two minutes or two hours.

The result of Loving thoughts is aliveness and self-actualization. A more Loving perspective creates a more Loving reality. This way of perceiving bestows us with a sensitivity to the beauty and sorrow that we all share. That unification brings more ease and lessens conflict.

Loving thoughts underpin morality. Thinking with Love increases the likelihood that we will speak and act in good Faith, that we will lead with Compassion and accept each other in all stages of our growth. Loving thoughts make quantum leaps in Unity Consciousness a very strong possibility.

Loving. Think about it.

Back It Up and Reverse It

Sutra 33 in Book Two of the *Yoga Sutras of Patanjali* states:

> "When disturbed by negative thoughts, opposite [positive] ones should be thought of."

We are guided to replace the unloving thought immediately with a Loving thought.

This is likely: You're going to be on a roll with Loving thoughts. Your heart will be streaming golden energy to your mind, and you will be noticing all of your beautiful thinking . . . a friendly universe, humanity's goodness, the warmth you feel when you acknowledge that you're doing your best here and now. You're vibing high—for real. And then in the five minutes that it takes you to walk back into your kitchen, you find yourself thinking about how scared you are or how awful life can be in some way. It's a thought-crash.

And that's how strong the ego-mind is. So what do you do when you have a thought-crash? Observe the thought you're having, without criticizing yourself for having it, and then just choose a more Loving thought.

Don't get down on yourself for thought-crashing. You could even be amused when it happens. *Wow, that didn't take long to dip.* That's how the shadow works and it's a natural condition. Expect setbacks and slips. For years on end, even. Just keep coming back to the kindness within.

Bring your mind back to your heart and let the warmth of your heart chakra rise up to your mind to form more Loving thoughts.

You may need to do this 900 times a day. This is mind training, and it's the work of Love and liberation. Choosing Loving thoughts is the art of the heart.

You may have to change your environment in order to change your thoughts. It's not always easy to shift into higher-vibration thinking when you're in a low-vibe situation. Take a break, get some space, and breathe into your heart chakra. Or as my dad would say, "Leave the room so you can change your mind."

On a larger scale, you might have to leave the job or relationship. You can't think your way to safety or sanity, you may have to physically make a move.

See the Weeds

Choosing Loving thoughts over fear-based thoughts is not the same as "positive think." Positive think is the New Age specialty that shellacks over negative thinking with karma-friendly cheeriness. It's the classic spiritual bypass.

Choosing Loving thoughts is not an act of denial, it's an act of creation. It requires some skillful awareness. First you need to be conscious that a low-vibration thought is passing through. And you are able to notice it without letting it take you down. You see the mind-cloud, and then you focus your attention on the spacious quality of your heart. This takes practice.

Fear- or lack-based thinking: Old tapes looping about why relationships broke down. Thoughts that condone working in order to earn your rest. Comparing yourself to others. Assuming the worst. Reinforcing guilt. Spurring on self-hatred. Fear of the future.

What Qualifies as a Loving Thought?

> "Walking the path of Love is our highest duty since we have taken
> on this body in order to achieve Love. Live, breathe, meditate,
> move, sing, pray, die—in Love. Spread the message of Love, for
> Love is the goal of life. Let the whole world be circled in Love."
>   –Swami Sivananda

The purpose of heart centered thinking is to make our unconscious thoughts conscious and to raise the vibration of our thoughts so we create more ease and health in our lives and the lives of others. This is a beautiful form of mind training.

Loving thoughts are:

- life-affirming, encouraging statements that are generated by the heart.
- aligned with Loving Kindness and all virtues . . . inclusiveness, goodwill, harmlessness, Compassion for self and others.
- expansive and calming at the same time.
- Loving thoughts can be the antidote to toxic thoughts. They may simply be the opposite of the fear-based or lack thinking that you're becoming aware of. They are the heavenly relief to the egregious thoughts that, as *A Course in Miracles* puts it, "keep you in hell." Loving thoughts are the healed edition of the unloving scripts we've had on repeat.

Loving thoughts are:

- not generated by the ego personality or small self.
- not reactionary or rebellious. For example, we're not screaming at the world to retaliate harshly, "I'm SO worthy!" We're not convincing our inner critic—or anyone else—that, despite our wobbly self-esteem, "I am super sexy and deserve it all!" We can hear these kinds of emboldened but slightly frantic affirmations coming from our fragmented selves—it's an inner fight that just stirs up more pain.

"A lot of people try to counteract the 'I am not good enough' with, 'I am good enough.' In other words, they take the opposite, and they try to invest it. That still keeps the world at the level of polarities. The art is to go behind the polarities . . . to 'I am.' And 'I am' includes the fact that I do crappy things, and I do beautiful things."

   –Ram Dass

Breathe into your heart space, call your inner fragments to gather 'round to hear what Love has to say to them.

Loving thoughts are:

- personal and likely universal.
- Loving thoughts can be your own wording of something that feels like a Truth. Or they can be inspired by or drawn from other mystical sources and Wisdom teachings. But it's key that they feel close to you—no one else can tell you how to think.

PRACTICE
Choose Loving Thoughts

First you need to identify the weeds in the garden of your mind. And then choose the Loving thought that you want to nourish. Ask yourself . . .

ME:

1. What's one unloving, fear-based thought I have about myself?
2. What might happen if I allow this thought to continue?
3. What's a divinely Loving, kind thought about myself (that is in healing contrast to the unloving thoughts I just described)?
4. What will happen if I allow this Loving thought to continue?

WE:

1. What are the unloving, fear-based thoughts I have about other people (that are specific individuals or groups, known or unknown, past or present)?
2. What might happen if I allow these thoughts to continue?
3. What's a divinely Loving, kind thought about the people or groups I mentioned (that is in healing contrast to the unloving thoughts I just described)?
4. What will happen if I allow these divinely Loving, kind thoughts to continue?

WORLD:

1. What are the unloving, fear-based thoughts I have about the world and how life works—systems, organizations, structures, paradigms, overarching philosophies?

2. What might happen if I allow these thoughts to continue?

3. What is a divinely Loving, kind thought about the world and how life works (that is in healing contrast to the thoughts I just described)?

4. What will happen if I allow these divinely Loving, kind thoughts to continue?

3 Questions to guide your Loving Thoughts:

1. Do you believe this Loving thought is **true**? A Loving thought should feel real to you. Plausible. Doubt won't diminish it. Which isn't to say you won't doubt a Loving thought some days. But you have enough Faith in the thought to hold on to it.

2. Does this Loving thought feel **compassionate**? Does it help you or someone else to feel a greater presence of Love?

3. Do you feel **uplifted** and/or more heart centered when you say it aloud?

7 VIRTUES

1. **Divine Love: The ultimate inclusiveness.** Everyone and everything is in. Divine Love neutralizes energy and makes space for everything to be what it is—our Light AND shadow. We are from Divine Love, made of Divine Love, and we are here to return to complete awareness of Divine Love.

2. **Compassion: Mercy + Courage + Oneness Awareness.** It's the wish for all beings to be free of suffering—and the causes of suffering. Compassion dissolves judgment into Love and division into interconnectedness.

3. **Wisdom:** Always looks for connections, commonalities, and how to bring energies and situations together. Wisdom always leads to the Truth. If an idea doesn't benefit everyone, it's unwise. Wisdom is **beyond knowledge**.

4. **Forgiving:** The heart is for . . . **giving.** The heart is Forgiving. The Soul will always respond with Forgiveness. Every time. Forgiveness is a Divine Power—it restores Divine Order. **It's the heart's natural inclination.**

5. **Loving Kindness:** Warm, **unconditional friendliness**. We use our free will to express our Divine Nature. When we practice Loving Kindness with ourselves, our understanding of seva (selfless service) deepens, as does our capacity to be with the Light and shadows in others.

6. **Resilience:** Our ability to respond from the heart—from Love. It's not about toughening up or enduring more suffering—it's about **adaptability.** This is the energy of expansion—which propels us forward. And adaptability is the mother of courage, fortitude, and resiliency.

7. **Radiance: Our suffering alchemized into Light.** Step 1: The ego dissolves, which makes way for Higher Light to pour into us. Step 2: We begin to reflect that Higher Light! Radiance is the result of all the experiences that burn away our false sense of self and obstacles. And we become more aware of our True Self: Radiant.

7 VIRTUES

Chapter 19

BY VIRTUE OF LOVE

Virtuousness is the process of getting into alignment with your Soul.

What Is a Virtue?

Divine Love. Compassion. Forgiving. Loving Kindness. Wisdom. Radiance. Resilience. Also . . . Harmlessness. Joy. Generosity. Beauty. Inner Peace. Courage . . . all are virtues.

Historically and psychologically speaking, virtues are thought of as a moral compass, usually rooted in a healthy psyche. A heart centered perspective on virtue is that and more. Virtues are metaphysical. From a spiritual point of view, **virtues are qualities of consciousness**. Each virtue is a unique expression of the Light of consciousness—of Divine Love. They're not emotions, they are states of *being*.

Virtues are healing energies.

A virtue isn't something that we do. For instance, we can't "do" Forgiving like it's a how-to process that we pick up and put down. We have to allow the energy of Forgiving to flow through us and into our thoughts and actions. A virtue is meant to permeate all of our doings.

REFLECTION. Envision that your Soul is a brilliant sun, a sphere of dynamic, golden Light. It's the mother of all virtues, the pure energy of Divine Love itself (this is your True Nature!). And emanating from that orb of higher consciousness are powerful rays of Light. Each of those rays—those lines of energy flow—is a virtue. The mother virtue gives birth to individual virtues. Divine Love emits healing rays of Compassion and Generosity and courage . . .

. . . and here you are with your feet on the Earth, basking in this sun—your Higher Soul. Those rays of Light are always shining down on you. Our job is to remove anything that might be blocking our view and access to that Light. The most efficient way to dissolve those impediments—often fear, or greed, or selfishness, and all kinds of hang-ups—is to move toward the Light of the virtues, to aspire higher.

As we make moves to embody Loving Kindness and Beauty and Resilience and other virtues, then the densities in our energy field will begin to dissolve. Then we can relax in the full warmth of Divine Love and all its nourishing energy, free of obstacles. Becoming virtuous is really just a process of getting into alignment with your Soul.

To become more virtuous is to become your True Nature, to be intimate with your Soul, and to walk as Love in the world.

Religiosity and dogmatism create a warped concept of virtuousness. These magnificent Soul expressions get grossly reduced to "good" behavior in opposition to "bad" behavior. Then religion imposes that twisted morality on its followers as a reward system for divine favor or rewards in the after-life. This isn't virtue. This is a power trip.

Real virtue is capable of being fearless, is inclusive, and never performs for rewards from authority or any sources outside itself. And ultimately, virtu-ousness is not for anyone else to measure or quantify.

This is important to understand. Of course there is a universal morality—it's the north star of Love. But the mind can't plumb the depths of the heart, and the intentions behind others' actions often get distorted by judgment and projection.

We're in such a crisis of human division that true virtue is getting canceled as virtue signaling, and the cancelers of virtue are lauded as virtuous. Ultimately your intentions—for goodwill or ill—are between you and the Infinite.

Virtues are not something that you "do" or perform. They're not a behavioral system for earning your keep on the planet. Virtues are the Light of Truth that flows into you and out of you. To be virtuous is simply to reflect the divinity of life—Light bouncing off of Light to create more Light.

Virtuousness is self-realization.

Spiritual Maturity

There's a developmental arc of consciousness and spiritual maturity that carries us from innocence and ego-directed morality—we could call this intellectualized morality—to a higher awareness of inclusiveness, where we truly embody virtues.

The unhealed self will front virtues as a means to get what it needs—attention, Acceptance, comfort. Virtue frontin' is actually a vice, but we'll get to that in a minute. The heart doesn't play that game. Your Higher Self Loves for the sake of Love.

There's a maturation process for most of us in terms of coming into alignment with virtues:

1. Metaphorically speaking, when we're at a kindergarten level of consciousness, we make the correct, moral choice based on if we

think we're going to get punished for the wrong choice. We learn to "not be bad" based on the judgment calls of those around us.

2.   As we evolve, we may choose the right action in order to please and thus to not be punished by a higher authority. That authority can be a societal or spiritual one. Wanting to please an authority whom we respect isn't altogether a bad thing. And emulating an admirable person can be a means to growth, for sure. But ultimately our Wisdom has to spring from within ourselves.

3.   If we continue to evolve our consciousness, eventually we'll choose right action from a place of *oneness awareness*. This is **Love for the sake of Love.** Our bearings point to universality, and we know that the right choice always considers the benefit of all beings.

In summary: At first, we do good so as not to get punished. Then we do good to please the authority that we respect (or fear). Then we do good because we feel connected to the divine nature of life. Our morality includes the good of *all*.

Standing Under the Light

We gradually awaken to what true virtuousness is. To understand means to *stand under*. This has such a beautiful application in terms of virtues. To understand a virtue is to stand under its Light, to become a receptacle of that higher energy.

We can have an intellectual understanding of a virtue. Let's take the virtue of Generosity as an example. Maybe we make donations, and we gift those in need in our neighborhood. We probably Love helping out our close friends. Giving makes good sense, and we play with it—within our comfort zone. So far, the virtue is a concept that we're experimenting with. We're testing how beneficial it is to our lives.

And sometimes the benefits of a virtuous behavior tempt us into using it to get what we want. We give for good PR and to polish our halos. We flip the giving into taking and, well, we know how that usually turns out. Emotional manipulation eventually backfires.

But when we come back to our hearts, we're more ready for Love than ever.

And that's when the Light of a virtue really seeps into our cells, and we want to act on it in more ways. The intellectual concept has progressed into a feeling.

Virtues dissolve preconceived notions of who is and isn't "deserving" of our Love. Virtues know that *everyone* is deserving of our Love.

Life then pushes the parameters of our Generosity. We may be called to give more of the little that we have. We may be invited to give to the people who extracted pain from us. Or maybe we're guided to give quietly without any expectation of praise. We give for the sake of giving. We give because we're beginning to identify with our divinity, and sensing the unlimited nature of our Love, we just become truly Generous. And it's euphoric—like standing under a golden sun shining Love into every layer of you.

> "Virtuous behavior is not about doing 'good' because we feel
> we're 'bad' and need to shape up. Instead of guilt or dogma, how
> we choose to act can be guided by wisdom and kindness. Seen
> in this light, our question then boils down to, 'What awakens
> my heart, and what blocks that process from happening?'"
>   –Pema Chödrön

So then . . . What awakens your heart? When do you feel greater than yourself, bigger than your daily identity? When do you feel close to other people or made of the natural elements?

Maybe it's when we imagine that the woman on the street holding out her hand for change is someone's sister. Or when our significant other comes to us vulnerable and tender, and we meet them with total presence. Or when we feel that *all* children are our children. When the news makes us weep. When we feel Mother Earth in our marrow and lungs, behind our eyes, vast as the sky.

Doing what awakens your heart and removing blocks to that process is, in essence, what it means to be a spiritual grown-up.

Vices Are Faux Virtues

A virtue used for emotional manipulation becomes a vice. Think: shifty branding and greenwashing—when companies do a little eco-friendly posturing to distract from their big environmental sins. Think: leaders feigning Compassion who are just trying to wrest control. Think: war and punishment in the name of God.

> "A vice that is a degenerated virtue is powerful because it draws energy from higher centers where the roots of virtues originate. Thus a virtuous person, when he turns into a person of vices, becomes dangerous."
> –Torkom Saraydarian

Vices start off as virtues, just like villains were once good guys. Darth Vader is just a heartbroken Jedi. To save his beloved wife from death, he gave his energy to the dark side, contorting something pure into a weapon for oppression.

Harry Potter's nemesis, Voldemort, was originally a tender-hearted orphan named Tom Riddle. His "half-blood" status—part wizard, part human—could have been a force for healing. His abandonment pain drove him to madness, and he used magic to feed his shadow.

The Wicked Witch in the Wizard of Oz was a social outcast because she Loved the wrong boy. Lucifer was an angel who felt rejected and then projected it on to God.

Unhealed sorrow can fester into blame, and blame can drive power struggles. When we turn away from the Light of the Soul, we can become vulnerable to lower vibrations. The fragmented mind gets hijacked by power lusting, and the original virtuousness is fashioned into a weapon for control.

The darkness grieves the Light, like the ego grieves the heart.

•

Virtuous behavior doesn't make anyone more "worthy" or valuable than anyone else. One of the most twisted misuses of a good quality is to lord it over others as a superiority. (See: eons of organized religion.)

That feigned superiority is wielded to divide nations—the harm that "holiness" has wrought—and devastate a life's work.

And there's something even more insidious that happens when the ego-mind uses virtues to feed on. We mash up virtue aspiration with worldly ambition and our small self, and we turn our lives into a self-improvement racetrack.

Aspiring to be more Generous or Forgiving requires some stretching and sacrifice, for sure. But virtuousness should never feel like a transaction to earn our place on the planet.

Real Virtues Extend to Everyone

Virtuous thought and action have to include everyone or the virtue isn't full-fledged. Virtues are an "all in" proposition. Virtues aren't exclusive in any way or dispensed only to our kin or the cool members in our club. If our Loving Kindness stops at our town borders or happens only with our own church folk, then we're still dim to Love. In that case, we're just half-assing Acceptance. The sun doesn't segregate flowers and bees or conservatives and criminals—it shines on all of us. Love is Love is Love.

Virtues are the only thing worth striving for, really. Nothing is more real or required or endless than all-inclusive Love. All other striving is a distraction on the path to higher consciousness. And when we aim for Love, the striving gives way to a state of receptivity. We're letting energy flow into us from the higher realms.

Aspiring to virtues helps to break down the blockages to the Soul. It's a win-win. The higher vibration of Love melts the lower vibration of the ego. Love really is the greatest liberator.

We can study and meditate on virtues, in earnest really lean in to the ideas of Compassion and Goodwill. And day by day, conversation by conversation, and relationship by relationship, we can practice and express those beautiful energies. And eventually *we will* embody virtues. It's Love's eventuality. It's the spectacular process of our awakening. Loving Kindness will be the tone of your voice. You will use Beauty to envision what's possible. Generosity will get baked into our economies and Forgiveness into our communities. You will bring Radiance to your friends' pain and every space you enter.

And when the Light is temporarily dim, you'll be Compassionate with yourself and your neighbor . . . making way for more Light.

It's this simple:
just truly, deeply intend
to be Loving.
And then ask your heart
for help to be that.
And then do what
your heart tells you to do.

Chapter 20

DIVINE LOVE

Divine Love Is the Ultimate Inclusiveness

It's all-encompassing, enveloping, *embracing*. Nothing is banished, condemned, or abandoned. Everything is in—all of your Light and all of your shadow. Divine Love is infinite.

And . . . *everybody else's* Light and shadow is ALSO all in. We radiate the Love outward to include our parents, family, and communities. Their judgment, their prejudices, the hurt they may have caused . . . it can all sit under the rays of Divine Love.

We push out even further, and we extend Love to people we don't know, to people we don't agree with, to people who have done glorious things and awful things. ALL. IN.

We emanate the Love even further. And we Love all of sentient life! Animals, plants, Love for the mineral kingdom . . . We push it out even further, and we Love what we haven't even conceived of yet. We Love the possibilities, we Love the mystery. We pour Love onto everything that comes into our view, that crosses our mind. We accept it as is. We see it as a part of ourselves. We wish the best for all. Divine Love is all-inclusive.

I've never been down with the theory that you have to Love yourself first in order to Love somebody else. Would it be ideal and highly efficient? Yes.

But since we're all one, what does it matter where the Loving begins? Even someone in a state of self-loathing can feel Compassion for someone else. In fact, it can be that very experience of warmth and sympathy for another that awakens us to more gentleness with ourselves. If even in our own despair when we muster Compassion for another, we ourselves expand in that moment.

Giving Love dissolves our ignorance.

Divine Love Is Everywhere

Always, omnipresent. It's like the sun—continuously generating life force, constantly radiating Light to absolutely everything in its realm. The sun never discriminates against whomever gets to bask in its Light. It just shines. **Love never withholds itself from Loving**. Divine Love is limitless.

Divine Love Is Fearless

> "The more you are motivated by Love, the more
> fearless and free your actions will be."
>   –His Holiness the 14th Dalai Lama

Fearlessness allows us to greet people and experiences with curiosity and inclusiveness. This is how Jesus Christ Loved—everyone, everywhere, no matter what. His Love in action extended to the marginalized and villainized.

The courage of our hearts (the French word for heart is *coeur*) disregards popularity contests and political games to serve and protect all beings. A courageous heart extends Compassion to the cruelest among us and brings the meek and the disadvantaged to the front of the line. Not to win divine favor, but because we know that we are all connected, all equal, and all here to heal.

If we get triggered by someone's behavior and then condemn them, that's the shadow self. Can you stay open-minded-hearted even though you want to contract and lay judgment? Breathe into your heart, don't let your mind collapse into overthinking and blame.

Let's say your friend makes it clear that they think you're being irresponsible. Or someone at work cuts you off mid-conversation, again, and you feel some rage flare up in you. Then all the stories related to the anger start firing up. Observe the feelings, don't push them away. AND breathe into your heart so you can move the heat up and onward.

The call is to keep Love flowing in all directions. *I'm hurt . . . and still, I Love. I feel offended . . . and still, I send you Love. I'm heartbroken, and still, I Love.* Divine Love is unbreakable.

Divine Love Abides

What does it mean to abandon yourself? You neglect yourself in order to please others. You're quiet so you don't rock the boat. You don't eat when you're hungry, you don't take a break when you need to rest. You change your appearance to get respect. The false self gives in to the temptation to prove its worth.

Love yourself like God Loves you. Abidingly. No matter what. Stay with your Inner Child. Stand by your brilliance. **You're a child of the Infinite. Act accordingly.**

The illness returns. Speak to yourself: *I will never ever leave you.* You fly off the handle and feel shame. Speak to yourself: *I will never ever leave you.* There's a rejection. Speak to yourself: *I will never ever leave you.*

Care for your life, being, and body temple as things that are astoundingly sacred.

Divine Love Leads to Higher Truth

**In the heart space, everything is seen. No veils, all vastness.
So Divine Love reveals the Truth. It's revealing—and welcoming.
It sees it all and gives Love to what it sees. This is the essence
of how to be Loving.**

Divine Love Neutralizes

"Love is constantly creating future possibilities for the good of all
concerned—even, and especially, when things go wrong. Love
allows and accommodates everything in human experience, both the
good and the bad, and nothing else can really do this. Nothing."

–Father Richard Rohr

Many mystics speak of neutrality as an expression of enlightenment. Not to
be mistaken with cold detachment, neutrality is the energy of equanimity,
spaciousness, absolute Acceptance.

Whatever it is, it could turn out good, it could be bad, but it is what it is,
and we Love it all here and now.

That's neutrality.

Divine Love Is Transmutational

Love turns everything back into Love. This is the homecoming of the Spirit,
and this is how the transmutation happens.

We become intimate with true power, Divine Power, when we engage our
hearts. This is true nondualism. All of it is in. The banal and the beautiful.
The easy to Love and the inconceivable. And we do it with the softest touch.

Like breathing. Like LIFE holds us—with steadfast inspiration and respiration. Divine Love is primal and transcendent.

We can train in Love. Really, this is what we're doing every day on this planet. Some of us are skipping class, some of us prodigies. We can *learn* Love, we can *become* Love! We become skilled in Love by waking up to the common sense that we're interconnected with all of life. And the goal is simple: learn to be better at Loving.

With Love in your heart, body, and mind, we move into the state of "each-other-ness." We see our neighbors as each other . . . the clouds, our angel kin, our animal friends, the forests . . . we are all each other.

●

Divine Love—absolute inclusiveness—is the flowing substance of all joy and the medicine for all sorrow. It's the revelation and the refuge. It's why we exist and how we make life come to life. Divine Love is the Truth of who we are. May it animate us in every way. May we walk by its Light and magnify it everywhere we are.

I LOVE YOU

If we are actually made of Divine Love,
then what does it mean to say "I Love You"?
In the heart center, there's no separate "I"
or small self who is doing the Loving.
There's just limitless Love that holds us all together.

I think what we mean when we (truly) say
"I Love You" to another is:

"I am Love, gazing upon You."

It's as if our heart chakra is a searchlight
flashing on whatever's in our midst or mind.
Our Love consciousness shines on others,
sees them in their fullness, recognizes our oneness,
and embraces the experience.

Love sees Love everywhere it looks.

@DANIELLELAPORTE

Chapter 21

COMPASSION

Compassion Wishes for the End of Suffering

In Buddhist terms, Compassion is "the wish for all beings to be free of suffering and the causes of suffering." I Love how thorough that is. EVERYONE free of suffering AND the cause.

Compassion Is Mercy + Courage + Awareness

Mercy is *May you be spared suffering, even though you stepped out of line.* Mercy is *I hope you have it easier than I did.* Mercy is *I hope you can make a quantum leap.* You might find that your greatest spiritual moments were merciful ones—when you just let someone completely off the hook. Or when you, yourself, were shown Love and spared the consequences.

Courage is the fortitude the heart affords you. It's the galvanizing stamina born of Love. Your heart helps you to keep showing up.

Oneness awareness, even if it's just at a conceptual level, is understanding that we all come from the same source. Different brothers from the Divine Mother.

Compassion Is Judgment Transformed into Love

Compassion is the transition of going from "I am judging you" to "On second thought, I'm letting judgment go and choosing Love instead." When you dissolve the judgment, Love is waiting right there, for everyone involved—as it always is.

When you're transmitting Compassion, it may feel as if the original offense recedes from the main story line. Whatever you were tacking the judgment onto is no longer the big event. Compassion fills the scene, and it creates an understanding connection between you and whoever and whatever you were criticizing before.

Compassion rises above the myopia of judgment.

You could be addicted. Compassion says, *There are so many reasons to Love you.*

You could be a thief. Compassion says, *There are so many reasons to Love you.*

You could have lied, cheated, and left. Compassion says, *There are so many reasons to Love you.*

Compassion says, *You are not what you do, not what you did, or anything that's been done.* Compassion understands there are so many reasons to Love.

Compassion Melts Harshness

One of the most beautiful effects of Compassion is that it dissolves the ego's harshness. The shadow will scour every situation and the people involved for reasons to withhold Loving understanding: *There are rules. We agreed to this. You broke a promise. You owe a debt. You have inconvenienced others. The harm is unforgivable. This is absolutely right, and that is very wrong.*

Compassion Is Thorough

All virtues are all-inclusive. If we're not including everyone in our Compassion, then we haven't quite got it yet. Compassion isn't just for the orphans, it's also for the oligarchs. You apply it to everybody—not just the people you like who mess up, but the people who mess up that you especially dislike. Everyone warrants Compassion. *Everyone.*

Compassion Is Singularly Focused on Everyone

You can't have passionate self-interest and be truly compassionate for others at the same time.

First let's define "ego-driven passion" versus heart centered passion. Heart centered passion is akin to enthusiasm. Enthusiasm vibrates at a high level, and it's essential for manifesting things.

Ego-driven passion, which is to say, passionate self-interest, thinks and acts in terms of *my bucket list, my objectives, I need to have this in order to set myself apart.* Lots of "me," very little "we."

Compassion uses oneness awareness to do all its reasoning.

You can still be passionate about running your race and being one of the best in your field. But your heart's enthusiasm includes wanting everyone else to be successful as well. Compassion is always considering what everyone else is going through on the journey. Compassion is focused on overall cooperation instead of crushing the competition.

Compassion Changes You

Think about a time when you've been on the receiving end of Compassion. Someone totally let you off the hook for something that was your fault. Or they saw that you were hurting, and they went out of their way to give you a hand or comfort. They got it, they got you, and they did something kind about it.

"It's okay. I understand."

What happens when we experience Compassion coming toward us? We relax . . . into gratitude. And gratitude brings us into the present moment. And presence is where our true creative power is. So we feel empowered to

Love by the Love we were shown. That virtue transmission increases our willingness to go out and be Compassionate to other people.

Mercy always pays it forward.

Compassion Has Compassion for Lack of Compassion

You will have exquisite moments of Compassion for yourself and others (and by the way, those moments heal us on deep levels). And there will be days when you are knotted up with resentment and grudges toward others and your own self and body.

Maddie is in our Heart Centered Membership community. She shared with us that she has ALS: "It's not easy to always be in Compassion with it . . . When I'm there, I feel so good. How can I be *more there*?" You can have Compassion for when you're not having Compassion.

Compassion Looks for Similarities

> "Knowing your own darkness is the best method
> for dealing with the darknesses of other people."
>   –Carl Jung

I was driving through my East Vancouver neighborhood one night and got slowed down by some cops yelling slurs at some guys who were hollering the worst profanities back at the cops. It was a powder keg of awfulness. I was really upset and righteously grossed out at the same time. I didn't feel very compassionate to any of those bad actors. I just thought they were unevolved and disgusting.

In a few blocks, the shock adrenaline settled down in me, and I thought, *That police person might be a decent parent. And the handcuffed guy could have been a foster-care kid.* But I was still pretty jacked on judgment. It was hard to shake their base behavior. I drove home feeling righteous about all of it.

I tend to view everything that crosses my path as a reflection of my inner state or as a lesson to learn. Given that POV, I had to ask myself one of the most evolved questions ever: *How was I being just like those asshats?*

And I didn't have to think about it long. I keep my hostilities in check for social graces, but I can still feel lightning bolts of anger crack through me sometimes. And for me, it's always alarming and disappointing when my own emotional violence surges out of nowhere. A guy cut me off in traffic, and I burned a ridiculous amount of energy thinking about how extensive of a loser he must be and how everybody in his life must think he's an asshat. And that everyone he ever meets will see right through him. All because he sped up and drove ahead of me.

He coulda been a monk on his way to bless his mother in hospice. It doesn't matter. What matters is that if I'm really honest, there are times when I mentally beat the shit out of people in defense of a fragile sense of my small self. It's trip wired from my long-standing authority issues, which, upon closer review and a few spoons of humility, I've come to realize are really just fears around authority figures. And that probably goes back lifetimes. But back to those punks on the corner . . .

Connecting my inner rage to the cops' outer rage helped me feel Compassion for everyone. We don't express it the same way, and our emotionality looks like it has a very different impact on others, but even if it's just a relational thread to hold on to, it pulls us on to common ground for a moment—and it in that split second, we can choose a more Loving thought.

All possibilities and seeds of expression exist within each of us. All things that we see and experience in others are also present in us. How might what we judge outside of us be a reflection of us? From a neighborhood brawler or a peaceful monk, to an orphan and an oligarch. When we make that connection, everyone becomes the recipient of our Compassion.

Compassion Is Dignified and Highly Capable

Self-pity is the shadow side of Compassion. We can think that we're in self-care mode, but sometimes we're at a self-pity party for one.

The big problem with self-pity is that it's completely disempowering, we doubt or don't engage with our capacity to heal ourselves. When you're in "poor me mode," you don't see your wealth—the wealth of friends, of fresh air and clean drinking water, of a strong immune system.

The particularly uncomfortable part of self-pity is that it usually takes someone else to point it out to us.

There was a time when I was really physically sick, and I was feeling so sorry for myself. Mold poisoning, bronchitis, and an overtaxed immune system that made my mind fog. *Why did I create this? I'm failing at wellness. If only I didn't feel this way, I could be happy, et cetera* . . . I had to be redirected by a healer who gently said, "Why don't you address your self-pity now?" Wince.

I thought I was being all Buddhist and approaching my pain from the echelons of mindfulness. Nope. I was feeling really sorry for myself, and that felt really good. I was also pairing all of this self-pity with a lot of Netflix and gluten-free waffles.

But I can say this for myself, I did get to work on the self-pity right away. I dedicated my walks around the lake to that healing. I turned it into a conversation with Creation. "Spiritual guides and Higher Self, please transform my self-pity into resiliency. I release my self-pity and move into Loving awareness." Over and over again, around Trout Lake. After praying that prayer for about three days, I had a new attitude. I did not feel healed of my emotional pain, and I was still physically weak, but I was able to have a more honest conversation with myself—and my friends—about what I needed to do to heal. And it had everything to do with being genuinely Compassionate—and therefore patient with myself and the Universe.

Compassion isn't saccharine. It doesn't flatter in order to manipulate. And Compassion will never speak down to your pain or anyone else's. It's immensely respectful.

With the power of the heart, you can champion yourself without pity or delusion.

Compassion Loves Right Now

Is it important to have Compassion for ourselves before extending it to another? You know, fill up your own tank first?

The answer is yes, and . . . both. Buddhist teachings advise to apply Compassion first to yourself, then to your friends and family, then to the greater world, and then to your identified enemies, those with whom you are in conflict. It's a concentric circle of Love that anchors you.

Self-compassion expands our Loving awareness to include the collective, so yes, it's ideal if you've got it going on for your own self. But can you feel Compassion for a family that's hungry, even if you do not feel Compassion for your own physical illness? Of course you can. Can Loving someone or being Loved pull you out of the depths of self-loathing? It happens all the time.

Do we have to learn to maintain our own reserves of Compassion and realize our irrefutable worth? Yes, yes we do.

But being that we're all one, riding the waves of evolution together, does it matter if you Love yourself or another person first? Nah. Love them while you learn to Love yourself. That works. Or Love your precious self with deep resolve and then go full on and gloriously inclusive with others—that *definitely* works. Love us all simultaneously from the inside out and back again. It doesn't matter what inspires or evokes your Love. Love is highly effective no matter who or what you point it at.

Compassion Sees Its Reflection

In a lot of mystical, metaphysical, and spiritual texts, we come across the idea that we're all each other's mirrors. Everyone is a reflection of us. Yes, in the most divine sense, this is true. But let's refine this idea a bit to make it more helpful and applicable.

If I were to regard myself as an empath and if I were relating with someone with a narcissistic personality, then as a sensitive, sensing person, I'm probably not going to use the reflection theory to conclude that "by virtue of association" I must also be a full-tilt narcissist.

However . . . on some level, we are all mirroring one another.

What I could see is that within my own shadow, there are narcissistic seeds. Maybe just specks of narcissism, but there they are. And as someone who's going for Divine Love, it's my responsibility to pull those seed frequencies into view.

And that's the win: to understand. We're aspiring to see common ground. To take responsibility. To be able to look at the person we're in conflict with and say, "Oh, I've done that before," and relax in that shared shortcoming.

And from that understanding, we release blame—in all directions—and we become Compassionate.

PRACTICE

I've Done That Before

Okay. This is a fantastic shortcut to instant Compassion.

It's really easy. It's one sentence. It's this:

"Oh, I've done that before."

It works for approximately 92 percent of all misunderstandings and conflicts. (The other 8 percent of conflicts will require radical Forgiving.)

Step one: Someone's behavior causes you pain or upset.

Step two: Say to yourself, "Oh, I've done that before." You've probably caused someone else pain and upset. Maybe told a lie, let someone down. Cheated a little bit, rounded up the truth. Spoke out of turn. Flew off the handle. Like, I've done *all* that before.

Maybe it was years ago, before you were as enlightened as you are now. Maybe it was last week. When have you been "that" kind of person to someone else? And if not outwardly to someone else, when have you done this inwardly to yourself?

If you can see when and/or where else you've reflected the same kind of behavior that's got you ruffled now, you're going to be standing on common ground—which is where all polarity dissolves.

Chapter 22

WISDOM

Wisdom Comes from the Soul

True Wisdom is a function of the heart. Knowledge is the by-product of the intellect, which is often steered by the ego-mind. Wisdom does not depend on intellectual prowess or accumulated facts. Wisdom and knowledge can stroll hand in hand, but they are very different energies.

When used for good, knowledge creates civilizations, cures, and phenomenal human progress. Breakthroughs! Justice! Evolution!

The shadow use of knowledge can be demeaning and destructive. Knowledge gets brokered with wealth or political sway. It gets hidden; worse, it gets distorted. Groups get divided into aware or uninformed, fact-based or delusional. It happens with institutionalized education, across nations, and within families.

The ego-mind Loves to do more research and extract data. It thrives on comparison. Knowledge can be used as one-upmanship and emotional policing. Vocabulary used as a rapier to slay someone's feelings. Jargon spun to baffle and dissuade. Stern opinions repeated often and loudly enough to propagandize.

Knowledge broadcasting without heart centered intentions is just an ego trip.

Wisdom has nothing to do with how studious, skilled, well-known, or accomplished someone is. IQ has no bearing on it. Case in point: heaps of business leaders who've helped pillage the planet for profit. Wisdom neither relies on worldly life experience. Case in point: elders who've lived in the same village their entire lives, calling the planet's pillagers to task.

●

We can come across someone else's Wisdom that we connect with, and they could be an enlightened being whose guidance corrects our course. But even so, external Wisdom is a reflection of our own inner knowing—it's creating resonance with the Truth that we carry inside ourselves. The most accurate gratitude we can offer our teachers is, *Thank you for waking me up to what I already knew.*

We can study the masters and follow the path of our elders. And we still have to experience the Truth for ourselves. Without lived experience, there's no chance of accessing Wisdom to share—only knowledge and theories. Wisdom emerges from the ashes of the beliefs we set fire to. It's the prize from the relationships that showed us mercy and happiness.

That said, not everyone will gain true Wisdom from their victories and defeats. Some people are just accumulating more data on how to avoid what they dislike and get what they want—little more of this, little more of that, and they tinker with a formula for worldly success.

Wisdom defines success as a meaningful life, and it finds purposefulness in every interaction. This requires a Loving gaze and a more sane pace of life. It requires that we are able to drop into our well of silence no matter what's going on around us. And the natural evolution of that slowness and ease will be less craving for distraction culture.

Wisdom Transcends Identity

Have you met someone who had that beautiful Wisdom energy? You felt, if even just for a minute, that you were in a quiet chamber with them, being given a secret gift? I've felt that with a man in San Francisco living homeless. We sat outside the opera house, and he told me how to be a good parent. Maybe his Wisdom was informed by regret, but he seemed to be speaking from another dimension.

Sometimes my son's Wisdom would blow me away, and I'd think, *You're, like, twelve.* Yet his advice always made sure that everyone was treated with respect, even the bullies. I had a wealthy business mentor who told me not to bend and a shaman from a small pueblo who told me to bend so I didn't break. They were both right.

I've sat in auditoriums listening to spiritual lineage-holders who have millions of followers, and I left thinking . . . *Hunh, actually . . . not so wise.* I paid to hear charismatic Ivy Leaguers posture about the origins of consciousness, and I thought, *All posture, not much Wisdom.* I'd rather hear what the grandmothers and children have to say about life. No pretense, all Radiance.

Wisdom has no zip code, no income bracket. Wisdom lives in brave hearts.

Wisdom Will Always Unite Us

It's not about what you know. It's about who you include.

How to tell a wise idea from an unwise one? A wise solution speaks to everyone's concerns and benefits.

Wisdom is inclusive. It will always look to create cohesion, to find our common ground. How can we find ways to relate to each other? What are our shared interests and struggles? What do you and I cherish? How can we all benefit from this?

This is the ubiquity of the Golden Rule. It's 4,000 years old and appears in every known ethical tradition and religion on Earth: "Do unto others as you would have them do unto you." From Confucius to Pharaonic Egypt to Jesus Christ, it's the ethical tenet that unites us all.

Segregation is the antithesis of Wisdom. It's only ignorance that intentionally classifies and separates beings from one another—into tiers of privilege or degrees of deserving . . . based on body type, family pedigree, race, health choices, religious beliefs, or who we choose to Love. The ego will curate history, statistics, and scripture to rationalize dividing us from one another. Where Wisdom employs Loving Kindness to build bridges and Resilience. Wise, we stand. Divisive, we all fall.

We Take Our Wisdom with Us

What does the Soul carry on with?

You don't take your money or your personality with you when you die. It's only the expanded Wisdom that carries over. You can speak five languages and have a heap of charisma and phobias, but all the identity stuff gets flushed in between incarnations. Your pathway to the Universal Mind stays intact. The more adept you become at connecting with that Wisdom now, the more you can rely on that key to unlock other doors.

All experiences you've ever had that have expanded your awareness of your Divine Nature . . . that expansion never contracts. Like the Universe itself, we exist in a constant and unending process of always, inexorably expanding.

Wisdom Is Cultivated in Stillness and Silence

"You believe in thoughts, therefore you become easily confused,
and so peace is hidden. Behind the screen of mind is the
realm of unchanging awareness—silent, vast, and perfect. The
wise leave aside the incessant murmurings of the mind and
merge themselves here in the infinite stillness of being."

–Mooji

A Universal Mind exists that is accessible to each of us. Think of it as a meta-physical Library of Alexandria, written by the Omnipotent Loving Presence that created the multiverse. It's eternally relevant, timeless, and current. You don't need Wi-Fi to get to it, you need to calm your mind and listen with your heart. You're already plugged into the Light.

If you can't hear yourself think, you can't tap the Universal Mind. You are the Universal Mind remembering that it is the Universal Mind.

Wisdom comes when we clear the clutter of ignorance and illusion out of our minds. Like all virtues, it's the Soul Light that pours into us when we make room for it. We do that by living more reflectively. We sit quietly with big questions, and we keep ruminating for as long as it takes for the Light to infiltrate our thinking and being. We slow down to breathe. We get off the performance ride so we can get grounded in what really matters—Loving each other enough to make heart centered choices. Being reflective often enough and long enough to be guided toward the highest good and the most honorable solutions.

Higher guidance won't necessarily silence your fears and reservations about what needs to be done. You may get the assignment to be a voice for the voiceless or to rebuild a bridge that burned down a long time ago. We can't all be Joan of Arc on the big day: *I am not afraid. I was born to do this.* Some of us are just going to raise our hand from the back of the room to say, *So, like, I've got this idea . . .*

When you trust your Soul to guide you, you'll be given ideas that elevate your life and unify the world around you. Whether you're brazen or quivering with your mission in hand, your Wisdom will tell you to keep Loving.

Wisdom Rarely Gives Advice

You can't make someone else wiser (not really). We can soapbox, we can motivate, we can even convince people to see and do things our way. But even if someone chooses the more "evolved" action that we're suggesting, it doesn't mean that they've taken an evolutionary leap.

We all make choices from the level of consciousness we're at.

Wisdom isn't as much about the choice—it's about *what's inspiring the choice*. Two people could make the very same choice for very different reasons. One could be motivated by fear, the other could be coming from Love. One could be feeling coerced, the other, divinely guided.

If someone is vibing low (in your humble opinion), *convincing* them to choose your option doesn't necessarily raise them up to a higher level of thinking. Persuasion can be a false power that creates more trouble for everyone. Let situations be spacious. Present options, don't push them. Float your suggestions, like so: *You might consider . . . Would you be open to . . . If it feels right for you . . .*

And then sit back.

Of course there are times to go into rescue-mode and campaign hard for someone to wake UP. One of the benefits of shared humanity is that we get to save each other from groupthink, and cult leaders, and signing bad contracts. Friends are for common sense and interventions.

But mostly, our job is to live by example and offer options without dictating or zealous attempts at influence.

Our unhealed self can take others' nonconformity to our advice as rejection. We take not being heeded very personally. People following our advice can feel very affirming. *Never mind the karma or their free will, they have taken my advice and confirmed how smart I am! Me, so wise and helpful.* Keep your heart open and keep a few opinions to yourself.

Most importantly we need trust in the Wisdom of the other person—even if it seems nowhere to be found. We don't know the machinations of their Soul, what they've just come through, or what life has planned for them. Wisdom can be a winding path, and we each have to walk it our way. Plenty of fools have grown into wise prophets and great leaders.

Practice what you preach and hope for the best as far as others are concerned. At least, that's my advice.

Chapter 23

FOR GIVING

The Heart Is For . . . Giving

The heart is for . . . giving. The heart is Forgiving. We are here to Forgive.

Forgiveness is humanity's wake-up call of the century. But rather inconveniently, we aren't very well trained in Forgiveness. We're raised in punitive, justice-seeking paradigms and systems. Someone steals our lunch or puts a dent in our car, and all moral messaging would have us seek some kind of punishment for the perpetrator. Humiliate the doer of badness and acquire payback. Do it immediately and quite thoroughly. React and extract.

Imagine if we were raised to respond to all transgressions first and foremost with Forgiveness. How transformative would THAT be?! *Johnny stole my lunch. He must have been hungry. Let's make an extra sandwich for him tomorrow.* The planet would shift on its axis.

What do you need to Forgive within yourself?

Everything.

Who in your life can you Forgive?

Everyone.

It might be easier to understand the concept of Forgiveness if we use the term "offering Love."

Who's being vilified and demonized? *Offer them Love.*

Who has caused you hurt? *Offer them Love.*

Who continues to treat you poorly? *Offer them Love.*

Offering them Love (For giving) does not justify anyone's destructive behavior. It doesn't align you with wrongdoing. It doesn't feed the shadow side. Bringing a Loving point of view to *any* situation helps us see what's really going on.

We can offer Love to the "worst" among us. And when we do that, we'll come to a better understanding of the dis-ease behind the harmful behavior and the extent of change that's required to restore natural order.

Offering Love doesn't wipe the slate clean for a perpetrator. We don't personally need to worry about how anyone else's karma gets rectified. **The Universe brings all things into balance—it's law.** We all get what's coming to us—the trials and the grace. Eventually, everyone goes through the fire to turn their suffering into Radiance.

Forgiveness Is Our Most Natural Inclination

People around you might attempt to talk you out of being Forgiving. *You should take them to court. Do not let that slide. This is unacceptable.* That's our cultural deal, to retaliate and assume the superior position.

What's Divine Love going to do every time? Forgive. We're actually built to Forgive. We're designed to Forgive.

At what point does Forgiving become enabling? Never. Forgiveness only takes one person because the heart only perceives oneness. We don't Forgive to get anything in return. We don't Forgive to get an apology. We don't even Forgive to create more harmony. We Forgive because Forgiveness is alignment with the natural order of the Universe.

Forgiving Has No Expectations for Change

Somebody could experience the gift of our Forgiveness, the gift of our Lovingness, and it could be positively alchemizing. For many people, it's a life-altering experience to be Forgiven.

Someone could get our Forgiveness, and it could ricochet off them. They can't take the Love in, their ego is gripping so hard that they're in an "I am not worthy of your Forgiveness" story line.

We have to be mindful that our Forgiveness doesn't come with a hook. "I Forgive you. Therefore, you should change your behavior and never do that again." It's not for us to say if our Forgiveness is going to be transformative for the person on the receiving end.

You could Forgive someone. They could keep doing the hurtful behavior that doesn't work for you. You have a choice. You can Forgive them again and stay. Or Forgive them again and move on. But the Forgiveness still goes down. **Your responsibility to yourself is to take care of yourself as God would want you to.**

Forgiveness Abides

So how do you Forgive yourself for hurting yourself? With unrelenting, constant Compassion over and over again. You Love yourself like you would Love a beloved child who just keeps falling down. You pick them up. You don't admonish them for falling. You pick them up again and again and again and again and again and again and again until they get it. You're going to keep falling down. You're going to keep making choices that hurt you. And every time you make that choice, you're going to meet yourself with Compassion.

The shadow is deep and far-reaching, and illumination doesn't happen overnight. That's why we call this *practice*.

Forgiveness Asks for Forgiveness

Asking for Forgiveness from the people who you think owe you an apology is a type of miracle work. Of course, this is not always possible or appropriate. (Please check your Wisdom before you proceed with this.) But we might be surprised how often this kind of unicorn messiah miraculousness of asking for Forgiveness is actually very doable.

REFLECTION. The ex-partner, or the relative, or the friend or colleague who you've been holding a grudge(s) against for years? Bring them to mind. Okay . . . you may have good reason to be upset or hurt. But try this: What's one thing you owe *them* an apology for? They may have done ten (thousand) things to create drama between the two of you. They may even have devolved since you parted ways. But! What's the one thing that you did in the relationship that was not cool?

Ask for their Forgiveness for that one thing.

I know. Wince. *But they* . . . *But you* . . . But never mind. Your heart wants to pound out Love. You don't need to worry about their side of the street, you're sweeping up your mess to unblock your True Nature. And you're not doing this to prove how much more evolved you are than them (the ego is sneaky like that).

You can do this because they're human and you're human, and we're all just trying our best.

Grudges are heavy. Love is Light. "I'm sorry" is like sunlight on the withering leaves of your relationship.

●

Light Guilt + Shadow Guilt

There's useful guilt and drag-you-down guilt.

"Light guilt" is what we'd call our conscience. It's your Soul nudging you to clean up a mess and head back in the right direction. It says, "Did that feel good to do what you did? I don't think that felt good. So how about we go and clean that up so we feel more aligned?" In the context of integrity, healthy guilt serves a higher purpose.

Then there's shadow guilt. Shadow guilt is the ego's main strategy for keeping you up at night and tied in knots with worry. It's always saying, "You're not keeping up. You shouldn't have said that. Strive more. It's all your fault." All we need to do with shadow guilt is give it some Love. Hear it out, but don't believe what it says.

> "People get into a heavy-duty sin-and-guilt trip. They feel that if things
> are going wrong, it means they did something bad and they're being
> punished. But that's not the idea at all. The idea of karma is that you
> continually get the teachings you need in order to open your heart."
>   –Pema Chödrön

You know what self-Love is? Self-Love is seeing your less-than-awesome behavior and affirming that you're still a Loving person. And that's what atonement is. It's when you see that your mistake was just an error in thinking, not a Soul defect. And in that observation, you've helped convert the mistake into Wisdom, which will guide your future thoughts, words, and actions.

Forgiving Harmonizes

Forgiving someone doesn't necessarily mean that things go back to the way they were. Forgiving doesn't have to mean that you're jovial, chummy, or "better than ever." When you've Forgiven, nothing needs to be forced, you're relaxed into your heart.

Forgiving means that we can create a new situation for everyone in a working balance. Harmonized. Harmony could be that you decided to just see each other once a year. Harmony could be, you text them every Sunday, and they rarely respond, but you feel alright about it. Harmony could be that the other person is ecstatic that you're back on track and you feel like you're back to square one—but you're at peace with it.

Forgiveness Isn't Overly Interested in Accountability

How do we Forgive someone but still hold them accountable? Well, why do they need to be held accountable? For our growth and peace of mind, or for theirs? It's a question worth asking.

How do we stay true to our moral compass as opposed to just sweeping something under the rug in the name of Forgiveness?

Forgiveness isn't in denial, and it doesn't have amnesia. Forgiveness goes like this: "That happened. I'm clear about what happened. I'm clear about the effects of what happened. And my Loving awareness can hold all of what happened. I see what happened, and I choose to Forgive." And the Forgiving reframes what happened.

Pre-forgiveness: *He cheated on me. Douche.*

Forgiveness: *He cheated on me. It was painful for everyone. It was a cry for help. This is all learning.*

You can recall the infraction but remember it through the heart. The heart has a multidimensional memory.

PRACTICE
The Ho'oponopono Prayer

> I'm sorry.
>
> Please forgive me.
>
> Thank you.
>
> I love you.

This is an ancient Hawaiian prayer for reconciliation and Forgiveness. Ho'oponopono translates to "correction." It's typically taught as a prayer that you offer to other people in the spirit of apology. And that's a beautiful way to work with it.

But here's an additional suggestion, which is how we work with it in our Heart Centered Leaders Program: offer the Ho'oponopono Prayer to your Inner Child or unconscious self. It's a very intimate and healing conversation.

You might be moved and amazed by what surfaces for you when you say, *I'm sorry. Please Forgive me. Thank you. I Love you*, to your shadow. You may see all the ways that you have neglected yourself or robbed yourself of opportunities for kindness or rest.

By reconciling our own unloving behavior with ourselves, we move into the vibration of harmony. And from that place, we can move into right action with our outside relationships.

Sing it, chant it, whisper, or enunciate. Cycle through the Ho'oponopono Prayer 7, 21, or 108 times and give your shadow all the Love you have to give.

The heart is

for

giving.

The heart is

forgiving.

Chapter 24

LOVING KINDNESS

Free Will + Our True Nature = Loving Kindness

Our True Nature is Love itself, but we choose whether we're going to express that Truth or not. It's a spiritual democracy. We can shine, or we can dim down in denial.

Loving Kindness is using our free will to express our True Nature. It's the decision to Love.

Loving Kindness is the highest choice we can make in any situation.

Also known as maitri in Sanskrit or metta in Pali (the sacred original language of Buddhism), Loving Kindness is defined as "benevolence, friendliness, amity, goodwill, and active interest in others."

Loving Kindness feels like the younger sister of Divine Love. She's the best friend you could ever have.

Years ago now, in the middle of a divorce, I was crying with a friend about my heartbreak. Specifically, I was lamenting that after all the months that had passed, I couldn't believe that I was still crying about my heartbreak. Bindu from Brooklyn (yep, she's a Buddhist) said to me, "Dude, you need some metta for your poor self."

I stopped to sniffle. "I need some metta all right." Sniffle. "What's metta?"

"Metta is kindness. It's your true nature. The Buddha taught that our true nature is '—and she said this very slowly to me, like a kindergarten teacher,—' warm . . . friendly . . . and luminous." MET-TAHHHH.

I wrote it down. And with that, I became a student of Loving Kindness. And what I learned was that, by being friendly to my hurt, my heart began to blossom and open to more people around me. Directing kindness to my afflictions distracted me from blaming whomever I thought was responsible for my pain.

As I tended more gently to my woundedness, I got close enough to see all the judgments I had about my loneliness and hurt—a lot of which I just projected onto other people: "You can't meet me where I'm at. I'm doing more of the work . . ." Those interrelational dynamics may have been accurate, but they began with me, and they could end with me.

It goes without saying that Loving Kindness is the process of a lifetime.

The warmer I got with my messy behavior and sloppy sadness, the more Compassion I felt for other equally unevolved human beings trying to find their way through the beautiful mess of relationships. The closer you get to yourself, the more you realize that we're all in this together.

"Each human being receives from God the gift of free choice by which he can make changes in himself and his world environment. This very power of free will is an expression of the image of God in man."

–Paramahansa Yogananda

Loving Kindness Is Inviting

Whereas Divine Love is fiery and transmutational, Loving Kindness is . . . warm, friendly, and luminous. While Divine Love is the magnificent, sweepingly inclusive state of consciousness that is the fabric of life itself, Loving Kindness is more like a distillation of Love: it cares very specifically about our hardships. Divine Love says, *Rise! You are the Eternal Light of the Great Omnipresence!* Loving Kindness says, *Need a hug?*

When we're not connected to our heart, we find it easier to be angry with other people. The ego-mind labels all things as separate, but **you are part of all the things that you should Love.** Loving Kindness is our natural ability to be *inwardly kind* . . . to help ease our suffering, and the suffering of others.

Being hard on ourselves is a reflex. When our inner critic is shredding us, Loving Kindness speaks to us like we would to a child that we adore. Steady, clear, affirming. It blesses all those parts of ourselves that we've abandoned—the fragments—and brings them into the heart center to be healed. This is only possible because it's not judging the parts. Our fly-off-the-handle part. Our double-checking-everything-obsessively part. Our feeling-sorry-for-ourselves part. Those parts don't have to shape up before they get given Love. They're Loved the moment we become aware of them.

Loving Kindness Avoids Laying Blame

Buddhism offers five factors for communicating with Loving Kindness:

It is spoken at the right time.
It is spoken in Truth.
It is spoken affectionately.
It is spoken beneficially.
It is spoken with a mind of goodwill.

A scenario for Loving Kindness: Let's say that you went out of your way to cook a friend's favorite meal and you're really excited to see them. But they show up an hour late and a bit baked. You're seething a little bit inside. Before you usher them into your house, you say—to make a point just in case they haven't noticed for themselves—"You're late, and you're a mess. But I Love you, so come on in."

Loving Kindness just says, "I Love you. Come on in." It never puts in a hook. It never lays blame, even when it's obvious that there's pain.

I know, I know you have boundaries, and you followed a recipe to make dinner. And your friend really does need to get it together. It's okay. Just breathe. Into your heart. Soften. And here's the move that changes everything: welcome in your frustration and your friend.

Now what about speaking out and clearing the air and all of that healthy communication protocol? Shouldn't we let our friend know how pissed we are about their lateness? It depends.

Let's keep in mind that the wounded self will try to justify spreading its pain around by any means. So someone can say their piece on the basis of open communication or being "someone who speaks their mind all the time." **If it's not connected to the heart, speaking one's mind all the time is irresponsible.** It's an outburst from the subconscious, and it's usually what leads to all kinds of local and global trouble.

Why do we need to share our thoughts? This is a monumental question. Roll with me for a minute . . .

I'm not suggesting that we repress our emotions. Communication in relationships is what the heart is to the body: it keeps life force flowing to the entire system. Speak! Commune! Connect! Reveal!

But do we need to articulate disappointments about the other person on a regular basis? How helpful is it really to let someone know that they let us down? Of course, there are situations when it's profoundly helpful, it can illuminate ways for us to grow.

But . . . do we really need to hold up someone's failing to them? Especially when that apparent failing is usually based on our very subjective interpretation of the situation?

Here's what I'm saying: the world will be a better place when we stop going out of our way to place blame.

●

I was at a party with the late, great author and 1960s counterculture hero Ken Kesey (he wrote *One Flew Over the Cuckoo's Nest*). Our friends introduced us by saying, "This is Danielle, and she just got engaged. Ken, why don't you give her some marriage advice!" He didn't miss a beat.

"Don't say it," he said.
"Don't say what?" I said.
"Just don't say it."
"To who?"
"To your partner," he said.

Kesey got through to me telepathically because it clicked, and he saw it dawn across my face. Don't say the thing you want to say that could be the hurtful thing—as much as you think you need to say it.

We nodded in silent, grinning unison. "It's all the things I *didn't* say to my wife for thirty years that kept us together."

Not saying it is easier said than done. But let's go back to the question. When we're disappointed by someone else . . .

Why do we need to share our thoughts?

Is it spoken at the right time? Is it spoken in Truth? Is it spoken affectionately? Is it spoken beneficially? Is it spoken with a mind of goodwill?

Refer to your heart, and Loving Kindness will always choose the right words.

Loving Kindness Holds the Criticism

Loving Kindness meets the situation without judgment, without criticism, and without cynicism.

Can you do that . . . for yourself? The next time you're berating yourself for saying, or eating, or doing the "wrong" thing, try skipping that berating part. Go straight to the Loving Kindness part where you show Compassion to the pain that happened from saying-eating-doing the wrong thing.

Then try it with someone you cherish. Maybe they say something that felt hurtful to you. Instead of pointing out that you think that they're being insensitive or wondering out loud why they did that thing yet again . . . what about not dishing out the cynicism and staying centered in the *heart* of the matter? Could be as simple as saying, "Ouch, that hurt." Just pure honesty that isn't barbed with your own self-judgment for being upset or judgment toward them for a moment of unawareness. Might be a disaster averted and two hearts softened.

We Can Train in Loving Kindness

Loving Kindness cares about and wishes wellness for another being, independent of agreeing or disagreeing with them. Loving Kindness wants nothing in return. It has no fine print, no desired payback. It gives Love to whatever's in front of it. Loving Kindness is really the capacity to sit with—and accept—the Light and shadow in ourselves and others.

It's Loving Kindness that can stop an emotional tsunami. **There's no modality to learn. It's simply the warmth within us.** So maybe you don't need another therapy session (or self-help book). Just take a few gentle breaths, in through the nose and out through the nose, and be very friendly with what's inside of you.

This kind of Love has a redemptive quality that pours forth from the heart. We can train in this energy, learn to glide with it, and direct it. Pain presents itself, and rather than getting down on it, we say, *Hello, let me hear what you have to say. Take your time.*

Addiction? Meet it softly, without judgment. *I Love you, no matter what. Today, tomorrow, and every day after.*

Obsessive neediness? *My heart is nourishing. Come in to be held.*

Neurotic controlling? *It's okay. You can be yourself here. Relax if you want to.*

Feeling shame? *Sweet shame. Sit in my heart. I'll breathe with you until you melt into Love.*

We train ourselves to meet—and transmute—everything with Loving Kindness. And that's how we come to realize that we are not our addictions or our challenges. We're something much bigger . . . and luminous.

Loving Kindness Is How We Take Responsibility for Our Life

"True metta [Loving Kindness] is devoid of self-interest. It evokes within a warm-hearted feeling of fellowship, sympathy, and Love, which grows boundless with practice and overcomes all social, religious, racial, political, and economic barriers. Metta is indeed a universal, unselfish, and all-embracing Love."

–Acharya Buddharakkhita

Think of a parent. They're completely in charge of every aspect of their child's well-being—nutrition, safety, play, affection, learning. They look after everything with Love and willingness. In the same way, we can use Loving Kindness to tend to *every aspect* of our lives.

Do all that you need to do to be well, with Love.

Loving Kindness Asks for Help (It's Also the Course Correction for Burnout)

This is what I've heard from so many people, women in particular, who've been grinding for success for so long: *I was never an anxious person, and now I'm having these waves of panic. I can't remember the last time I slept through the night. I want to get rid of all my things—it just doesn't matter anymore. I want something I can know for sure. I'm longing to be held by life. I'm obsessed with thoughts of losing my partner, my kids, of death. I need to nap . . . for six months. I want to start a commune with my friends and some chickens.*

And my response is: *Good news!* It's all a wake-up invitation. All the painful realizations and yearnings are memos. Your heart is requesting more Soul alignment—and maybe even chickens. And alignment with our Soul requires Loving Kindness. And sometimes we need to find that in community.

The medicine for burnout is rest, support, and receptivity. All of which can be mystifying for high performers. But no more white-knuckling it, okay? Meet yourself where you are, observe your longings, and Love yourself enough to ask for help when you need it. And we all need it.

Loving Kindness Opens Us Up to Serve

The practice of Loving Kindness is the greatest honor you can pay to your Soul. How can you measure the circumference of that higher Love? With your helpfulness. Your inclination to be inclusive of others will increase. It will happen organically. When you meet your own challenges with kindness you dismantle internal hate and scarcity programming. The Loving Kindness—our inner divinity—is bigger than the challenges we face in the outer world. Rather than being propped up by grand identity masks and audacious goals, **we can become much more powerful simply by being Loving people.**

Go metta every way you can. Dance and dedicate every sway to your beloved—they don't even have to know about it. Dedicate your yoga practice to all people recovering from injuries. Swim in a cold ocean as an act of thanks for Mother Earth. Do healing acts in support of your closest friends. Like when one of my girlfriends texted our group chat to say she had an infection. We all drank extra water that week on her behalf—just close your eyes and send the healing benefits of whatever you're doing to where you want it to go. Light a candle, eat a meal, go for a walk tonight, and dedicate the merits of that practice to the benefit of all beings everywhere.

Metta metta metta everywhere.

When you practice Loving Kindness, you're creating an infinity loop of vitality. First of all, you will feel more connected to the world around you. With a more pliable heart, you're going to empathize with the concerns of mothers everywhere. You'll relate to the courage of crocus flowers cracking through snow in spring. The heart connections and revelations will vitalize you. And your vitality becomes a form of service to the world.

And because that vitality springs from the connection to humanity and the elements of life, your concepts of "self" and "other," and "giving" and "receiving," will fuse. And you'll be holding the seeds of *seva*—"selfless service"—in your heart. And very naturally, you'll plant that Loving Kindness everywhere you go.

Loving Kindness Leads to the Ultimate Strength: Gentleness

Gentleness is the fruit of our spiritual labor. Loving is the work that really *softens us*. We become more accepting, more pliable. More . . . *heart centered*.

Gentleness was a revelation for me. I'd always used my spiritual practices to cultivate *discernment*. So, for instance, I used meditation as a tool to *more clearly* see into situations. I approached all forms of cleansing as a means to having more insight into people, into life, into myself. And meditation and cleansing certainly helps us get to clarity. But it's gentleness that helps you do good things with your clarity.

The spiritual teachers that I most resonate with have a fierce gentleness. Their caring has a parental nuance. They don't flaunt superiority or overregulation. Instead, they teach with profoundly gentle, unwavering attention. They embody Loving Kindness. And for me, *that's* why it's healing to sit with them and their teachings.

I've finally learned to talk to myself like an awesome friend. "Oh, Danielle, look at you, you're suffering." And then I say back to myself, "Yeahhhh, suffering . . . sigh." And I let myself have that moment. And then not too long after—could be that very moment or the next morning—I compost that sympathy into some counterbalance. I gave myself the Loving Kindness that I needed, and that ends up fueling a better mindset or healing action to move out of the suffering funk.

Gentleness stops the fight, grounds the flight, and thaws the freeze reactions. By being gentle with yourself, you set your nervous system at ease. And **when you relax, solutions come.**

We can't make real gains when we're being ruled by fear. It may look like progress on the outside, but fear creates involution, not evolution. Anything we do out of coercion or fear of loss usually leads to a wake-up call or a do-over. **You will make more progress by being gentle to yourself than you ever will by being harsh.** For most of us, Loving Kindness will be the greatest personal breakthrough of our lives.

PRACTICE
Dedication of Merit

> Many ancient practices, Buddhist, Hindu, and others . . . have been offering *dedications of merit* for eons.

> **Dedication of Merit**
> We dedicate the merit of this practice
> (or meal, exercise, meditation . . .)
> individually and collectively,
> to the awakening of all beings,
> and the purification of the Greater Mother,
> our planet Gaia.

> Say this before and after your prayers or meditations . . . and to begin and end your workday (!) or your yoga, or grace with meals, or bathing, or a walk in the woods, making a donation, reaching out to a Loved one, working with a client, tending to a neighbor, mending a misunderstanding, before a moment of stillness or song or movement—making ALL we do an offering for ALL.

Chapter 25

RESILIENCE

Resilience Is Adaptable

Resilience has nothing to do with sucking it up. We don't need to get tougher or more leathery to be more successful. Resilience happens when we open up to our hearts. Think of a tripod. Closed, it tips over. Open, it's immovable. That's what the heart-mind is like. The more open hearted we are, the stronger we become.

> "The green reed which bends in the wind is stronger
> than the mighty oak which breaks in a storm."
> –Confucius

I traveled to the interior of British Columbia to meet with a medicine man. A cherished friend told me that he could help shift some energy for me. There was a lot of conflict in my life at that time, and I wanted some support and some spiritual warrior training. The source of that strength was about to come as a surprise.

He begins a healing ceremony with me, eagle feather in hand. I breathe deeply, a bit afraid of what might slip out of me. I'd been in a defensive posture for many months after some relationships fell apart. I was not trusting my own perspective as much. I'd become guarded against anyone who I thought wanted to extract something from me—energy, connections, too much of me.

I exhale, and then come soft tears. I feel so rooted into the Earth, it's as if my feet are made of soil. I can feel the grass growing. Expanding.

We go further into the ritual. As sage smoke rises, I feel the heaviness of the year lifting. The healer was pulling out whatever in me had calcified from contraction. To complete the ceremony, he calls again on the four directions, and we both speak our thanks to Spirit.

We held our places in silence for a long time. My heart felt vast, skylike, natural. He put his hands on my shoulders and crouched down to eye level with me and said, "The way forward is always to bend. We bend so we never break." I nodded, knowing it was a Truth and a new assignment. "We bend so we never break." I echoed.

Then we high-fived and smiled the biggest smiles. And just to balance out all that sublime sacredness, we went back into the house and drank Coke with apple pie and watched *America's Funniest Home Videos* with the whole family. Also very healing.

I was seeing that resilience was a dance and not a stance. I had to actively change my mind. I had to let go of what I thought the best outcome was. I had to loosen my grip on desires.

And I saw that I had to meet the extreme challenge that I was in with radical flexibility. Instead of armoring up, I had to create a more supple and awake response to everything that tested me. None of us are meant to be fortresses. We are created for connection—to the sweetgrass, to each other, to the Source of all things.

Resilience Is Your Capacity to Live from the Heart

"The conditioned reflex is whenever you encounter difficulty, whether
it's inside of you or whether it's in life, is that you leave the heart. At
those moments, the thing you need most is to live from the heart."

–Adyashanti

Resiliency is adaptable and inclusive. Resilience considers everyone's benefit.
She changes her mind. He lets go of overcontrolling. They pivot, resilient.

When you're living and leading from your heart, you give everything space
to arise, to appear, and then shift. We're adaptable to what's emerging. No
forcing, no sucking it up, no enduring. Rather . . . *adapting*.

Endurance versus resiliency is the difference between struggling to carry a
heavy boulder over a field . . . and then deciding to just roll it across.

This means that a key practice of resilience is to stop wishing for things to
be different than they are. We should hold inspired visions in our hearts
and match them with action. But the kind of wishing that wants to recreate
the past or envies other people's better fortune . . . that craving weakens our
higher will. When we can objectively assess a current situation, then we
can clearly see what needs to be done to move things forward—whether it's
triage, or a rest break, or a long-term plan.

Resilience Builds Bridges

The ego personality tries to wrest control over our higher nature through
exclusiveness. Who has access, who can come in, who's entitled, who
deserves what.

Here's the demise of exclusivity:

1. Exclusiveness blocks the flow of life force. When Love isn't circulating, energy blockages form.
2. Energy attracts its reflection. This is a universal law: like attracts like.

So, if we're running the energy of "exclusiveness," of restriction through our system, then we're going to attract more closedness. We'll start to feel stagnant. The more divisive we are with the outside world, the more bound up we're going to feel in our own selves. Too much ego and not enough Higher Love and we'll start to feel very, very stuck.

Too much time spent in that fenced-off, stuck place can lead to paralyzed will. You won't know where to go or how to break free. It doesn't matter whether someone is majoring in philosophy, living on a commune, or running a corporation. If they're slotting people into "worthy" and "unworthy" categories, they're going to feel that sorting and ranking energy come back on them. An uptightness. Lots of opinions start to roost. Lots of energy is burned keeping those opinions fueled. And that person becomes too brittle to bend—anything but Resilient. The restraint and control required to stay exclusive, closed, and in control is exhausting.

It's better to just open up your heart and let in other people and other perspectives. Inclusiveness stabilizes us. And when we're stable in Love, we're more courageous and Resilient.

> **Keep softening. Keep adjusting, Change the plan—daily if you need to. *What next? Is everybody okay?* You can Love and understand your way through anything.**

PRACTICE
Brihadaranyaka Upanishad 1.3.28

This is a beautiful prayer, even more powerful when you sing it into your heart center. The Upanishads teaches that these are highly purifying recitations.

Lead us from the unreal to the real.

Lead us from the shadow to the Light.

Lead us from death to immortality.

Chapter 26

RADIANCE

Radiance Is the Gift That Suffering Brings

Maybe you were thinking that Radiance was about our inner glow. And it is. Ultimately. But before we get there, we have to look into the nature of suffering. Stay with me . . . it will be worth it. Radiance always is.

This analysis requires some courage. At least, it has for me. Because as much as I want to transmit Divine Light, I have feared what's required of me to do so. What suffering might I endure to know my True Nature? Will life pile on the pain as a wake-up call? Will I press snooze on the wake-up call and create more suffering?

It reminds me of what the Zen teacher Alan Watts always said about suffering. "There will always be suffering. But we must not suffer over the suffering." And Eckhart Tolle, who teaches that challenges are for intensifying our presence, not for suffering.

If we criticize ourselves for suffering or slip into self-pity, then we unnecessarily compound the suffering. **If we resist the pain, we delay the healing.**

Eventually, we start *meeting* our pain with kindness. And this embrace is a kind of alchemy. The honoring of the pain transforms the pain itself. And that's when pain becomes power and the virtue of Radiance begins to glimmer.

Radiance Doesn't Look Back

Fun with suffering and Radiance goes like this . . .

Step 1: The ego dissolves to make way for Higher Light. When the ego experiences a crisis—a loss of a dream, humiliation, an identity in question—its self-centeredness begins to break down. This is a good thing. This crumbling allows one's True Nature—inner Light—to shine through.

It's in the crumbling and revealing process that our me-me-I-meeeee desires will disintegrate, and then our heart centered aspirations move into forward position. We reorient from "me" to "we."

Step 2: We begin to *reflect* the Higher Light. When we've been cleaned out of our old identifications as separateness and superiority/inferiority then we become a more reflective surface for higher consciousness. Essentially, we've just made it much easier for life to work through us.

Our personal shining is God shining through us. Radiance is our reflection of Divine Love.

> "It is by suffering that suffering is overcome,
>   because without suffering very few would see
>   the need for self-purification which leads to
>   the unfoldment of our immortal Self."
>   –Anandamayi Ma

There's relief to be found in this paradox: **"It is by suffering that suffering is overcome."** Once we experience the Light after the tribulation, there's no returning to our previous form. We are changed.

It's at this point that most of us make a vow to never go back to the way we were. *Nope, no way am I going back there again.* In our redemption, we commit to wakefulness. Our Wisdom and Radiance join hands. We will do whatever it takes to stay close to the Light and to bring others along with us. This is the time when the ego will back off, lay down the fight, and actually *allow in the higher frequencies.*

It's important to remember that the ego isn't submitting because we've been forceful or motivational with it. *Yes, it feels like life has pummeled us. But really, life has been decluttering us.* And the pliancy of the ego is the result of us learning to be gentle with ourselves. The victory comes through Loving our woundedness. Our attachments put up a fight, but after enough Love— being in nature, rest, community, doing what brings us joy—we've proven to our small self that we have the capacity to Love it.

Radiance Comes When the Facades Go

Truth is the fire. Our ego façades are the wood.
We emerge from the flames more aware of our divinity.
Radiant.

I was in the middle of a highly growthful romantic relationship (read: it was so messed up). Years of stressors and a few traumatic events had pushed my brain chemistry and hormones to the limit, which primed me for the first panic attacks of my life.

I was on a retreat with my psychotherapist, Anne, coming very undone. On a particularly rough day, I walked into the adobe, looked at Anne, and shook my head to say, "I'm not doin' so good." She walked toward me like a calm paramedic, grabbed a towel out of the closet, and said, "I'm taking you down to the river."

We walked downstream silently, and I made my way to the bank rocks. Knees and forehead pressed to the ground, I sobbed. Anne kept a hand on my lower back, and just at the right time, she laid the towel next to me and left me to be alone. I stripped down, stepped into the cold rushing stream. And I thought, *I am like wood right now. And life is the fire.* My emotional agony was severe. I felt like petrified wood, so heavy, being burned alive—which takes on a different meaning when you consider how Radiance happens.

There is a kind of pain that nobody outside of us can resolve for us. Not our best friends, not our lovers, not even skilled psychologists who know so much about us. Nobody. It's a brutal revelation that's the dawning of our greatest power. That we have the power to heal ourselves—when we turn to Source, which is already within us.

Our extreme pain has to be given up to Creation itself—it's the only remedy.

And that's what I was moved to do that day in the rushing cold water. I just gave my pain to God—along with my heart. *I surrender this unto you.* Of course I'd prayed for relief a hundred times before. But this time, it was an act of self-compassion and mercy. I allowed myself to consider that I was so supremely loved that the Divine was enthusiastic to ease my sorrow. That God was waiting for me to turn my densities and resistances over to the Light.

The beauty of baptizing oneself is that the blessing is done *through* you, not by you. We become conduits of Love.

The rest of the details—the tears, the flight home, the break-up-down-through—those aren't as important as what was coming next. My story from that point on involved a lot of Soul fire that burned my identifications down.

For months afterward, I felt electrical-like energy streaming through me. It was not the angelic embrace that I'd fantasized about. The energetic shifting was very destabilizing and disorienting. It ravaged my perspective of my "self."

I suffered terrible anxiety waves. I woke up thinking about suicidal plots. I had to press pause on being a public person. Actually, I had to pause being any kind of "person" that I used to be. Always a classic introvert who relished solitude, I went through weeks where I felt that I couldn't be left alone. I wanted to scrap the life plans I'd made, my ambitions seemed so vapid. I cried rivers.

My relationships felt tenuous—who was going to put up with me if I stayed in this state for an extended period of time? I felt that my spiritual infrastructure was shredding. I hid out at a small Catholic retreat center, sitting by the fire with a box of tissues, reading the works of Saint John of the Cross—the 16th century mystical priest who coined the term "dark night of the Soul." I was learning that the dark night reveals your Light.

It was about nine months of a "living death," as Anne called it. But day by day, with every choice that leaned toward gentleness, I healed. I healed precisely because of gentleness.

It wasn't so much that I "emerged" from the flames all victorious and glorious. It was simply that I was still standing after the fire. I had been reduced to my more essential self. And I had fewer expectations and more Compassion—for all of us.

In our most arduous life simplifications, we increase our capacity to Love. It's when we and our suffering call for higher guidance that Radiance comes through us.

"We find God by peeling away ourselves."
    –Father Richard Rohr

Radiance Rides the Changes

Experiencing tragedy and suffering doesn't change everyone—even though it should. That's what suffering is designed to do. We face down illness, we suffer heartbreaking loss, we recover from catastrophes. And in the center of the pain, so many of us beg for mercy. "God, If you get me out of this, I promise I will never . . ." Fill in the blank. "I will dedicate myself to this. I will never take that for granted . . . I will donate to . . . I will give my life over to . . ."

And for a while we do change our behavior and we live from the heart. Maybe we start telling people that we appreciate them. We become really good at emotional intimacy. We surrender to a greater plan.

And then a year, maybe two years later, we might find ourselves buried again in unhealthy habits. That intimacy that we were so good at? It just drifts. We fall back asleep. We move back to the familiarity of our small self. The personality mind takes over, and we're back to focusing on our bucket list and excessive self-concern. We're not begging God for anything anymore—in fact, we're not even talking to Spirit that much.

How do we make the Light "stick"? We avow to Love. We commit and we recommit.

Can we skip the suffering on our way to Divine Love? It doesn't seem so, but we can make friends with it and lessen the intensity. We get in front of the suffering by becoming more proactive with Love and all its virtues. The more steady we are in Loving Kindness, the fewer wake-up calls we'll need to answer.

Living the virtues burns off the energetic densities we carry.

Love dissolves fear.

Inclusiveness disarms greed.

Gentleness melts polarization.

Radiance starts as a spark, *an inclination toward your heart*. And with every act of goodwill, we fan that spark into flames. And this is the work of these times, of the Age of Aquarius that we're in: to intentionally fan the flames of Loving to a scale that benefits all beings.

●

After someone has passed through a portal of pain, there's a definitive "before and after" in our life, and we can't believe how blind or selfish or closed off we were.

"You already know that you are neither unworthy nor special (in the sense of pride). You know that neither of these identities signifies who you are, because ultimately both are unsatisfactory and lead to suffering.

The problem is that behind both of these masks lies not another or better or more spiritual mask, but the direct experience of no mask. And the direct experience of no mask is something that most people avoid with great resolve, because the familiar and morbid comfort of a known identity is preferable to being stripped down to our unknown Radiance."

–Adyashanti

Behind the masks and all the roles we play is our awareness of Truth—the Truth that we are sparks of the Divine reflecting back the Light of our origins. We're here to step out of the theater of the ego and into the boundless landscape of our true nature: living, breathing reflectors of God Consciousness in all that we do. *Radiant.*

PRACTICE
The Virtue Blessing

This practice was created by V.S., an energy healer experienced in many Wisdom traditions. She and I have been working together for many years to distribute meditations and create the Heart Centered Membership experience.

In this practice, we're blessing and offering virtues from our heart center. Heart centered offerings come from a place of nonduality and inclusiveness. So we understand that the "other"—people, relationships, places, communities, segments of society—is a reflection of us. We're offering our Forgiveness, release, and Compassion.

This practice activates and energizes core virtues within us so we can offer and radiate them to the world. You can do this anytime for the specific virtue you want to focus on or do the group of seven virtues in one practice.

Note: Lotuses in many cultures represent purity of body, speech, and mind.

1. Breathe and Om

Close your eyes and breathe fully and gently into your heart chakra.

Tap gently three times on your heart chakra.

Sound Om 3 times, loudly. Take an in-breath, hold for a few seconds in your heart chakra area, then on the out-breath, chant Om. You're infusing your energies with a cleansing sound current.

2. Infuse the virtue seeds

You can focus on one or all of these virtues:

Divine Love. Compassion. Wisdom. For Giving. Loving Kindness. Resilience. Radiance.

    a. See *one golden seed* at a time appear in your heart. (You can do this for one, a few, or all seven virtues.)

b. Take a deep breath into your heart, and on the exhale, *speak the name of a virtue into each seed*. You're breathing energy into every word. You're acknowledging the Truth, beauty, and power of that virtue. Optionally, you can **sound Om** after you energize each virtue seed.

c. You become aware that **your heart is filled and flowing with golden-hued Divine Light**.

d. Now you see this golden Light energizing the virtue seed(s) to grow into a **full, seven-petalled lotus blossom**.

e. **Ask your Higher Self to bless the virtue blossom(s)**. With strong intention: *Dear Higher Self (Higher Soul, or Solar Guide . . .), please nourish, expand, and protect these lotuses of Light.*

f. **Offer up the lotuses.** With each exhale, offer each lotus blossom out into your families, school, community . . . or the planet . . . or the solar system . . . or the Universe.

g. **Give thanks.** Conclude with a few deep breaths and give thanks.

Note: Choose whatever range feels natural for how far you extend each lotus. You could direct it to a person as you begin, and each time you do this blessing, extend the lotus farther outward until you're giving blossoms to the entire Universe. Always start small, and then keep going bigger. There's no limit to what you can bring into this practice or into your heart space.

REFLECTIVE LIVING

Chapter 27

CHANGING WITH LOVE

Faith is required for all shifts to occur.

What Is Your Antidote?

an·ti·dote, noun
: a remedy or other agent used to neutralize
  or counteract the effects of a poison

: cure, preventive, corrective,
  countermeasure, counteragent

The solution to our strife and pain is usually the opposite energy of what got us to strife and pain. Overworked? Work less. Angry? Be gentle. Feeling stuck? Move—your body, energy, ideas around. Exhausted? Rest.

That antidote usually feels like a strange and foreign behavior. Naturally. We're pushing against the personal culture we've created. We need to counteract thinking and actions that have been ingrained and habituated.

Whatever your healing antidote is, it has to be strong enough to burn through the resistance that will surface. You need to believe it will work. Another word for it: Faith.

Faith is required for all shifts to occur. Identify what your antidote might be, believe it has the power to bring you into balance, and then give it a chance to do its work on you.

How to Approach It

- What are you tired of feeling? What's the contrast to that feeling?
- What are you overdoing? What does doing less look like?
- What is inflamed or ingrained? What would cool that down and set the situation at ease?
- What's the "story" that makes the future look gloomy? What's a beautiful vision?

If you've been striving all your life to be better, perhaps your antidote is rest and Acceptance. You see that? The antidote isn't a fix-it plan, this isn't a sneaky way to strive harder. The antidote reverses and dissolves the harmful pattern.

If you've been letting fear hold you back from fulfillment, maybe the antidote is a combination of Compassion and conviction. You start being kind to your fear while making good on your promises to yourself.

If your cynicism and pessimism have pushed people away from you, maybe celebration is the medicine.

If defeatism is your poison, maybe you need to declare that you've already won—just by still being alive and truly kind after all you've been through.

Counterbalancing is what we're all being called to master. For our own healing. And to turn the global tides. Be the calm in the eye of the storm. Be the Wisdom that stands outside the hysterics, waiting patiently. Crack the best joke at the worst time. Extend the apology. When there's hatred in the dialogue, maybe you can prove the benefits of kindness and respect.

When everyone is hurling insults, find the one reason to be compassionate for everyone involved.

> "Where there is no Love, put Love, and you will draw Love."
>   –Saint John of the Cross

Counterbalancing takes incredible fortitude. We're looking at changing some bad psychological habits *and* the course of humanity. It's doable. Because the base ingredient in all antidotes is Love—of which we have an infinite supply.

PRACTICE
The Prayer Of Saint Francis

This is a magnificent prayer for becoming the divine counterbalance. You can speak this to your Soul or the God of your understanding.

Bear in mind the universal law: "For it is in giving that we receive." So we are taught by Saint Francis: "And it is in dying that we are born to eternal life." This isn't necessarily literal death. It's a dying of the old ways and our illusions of separateness. Awareness of our oneness is eternal life.

THE PRAYER OF SAINT FRANCIS

Lord, make me an instrument of your peace;

Where there is hatred, let me sow Love;

Where there is injury, pardon;

Where there is discord, Union;

Where there is doubt, Faith;

Where there is despair, hope;

Where there is darkness, Light;

And where there is sadness, joy.

O Divine Master,

Grant that I may not so much seek

To be consoled, as to console;

To be understood, as to understand;

To be loved, as to Love;

For it is in giving that we receive;

It is in pardoning that we are pardoned;

And it is in dying that we are born to eternal life.

Amen.

Soul Soup

When the caterpillar becomes a butterfly, there's a stage in its metamorphosis where it's completely liquified. It is a "nutritive soup of enzymes." You can't tell that it used to be a caterpillar, and there is no visible indication that it will be a butterfly. It's entirely unrecognizable.

There will be a watery passage to swim through on your way to balance. You won't really know who you are or what you're becoming. Anything could happen, could go either way. Something revealing, wonderful, or tragic, something miraculous, or epiphanic that sets you at ease. Your beliefs get pulverized, your dreams evaporated. It's the most unsettling time.

When you no longer recognize yourself, you have the opportunity to meet who you truly are.

Through this untethering, you're learning how to be Loving. How to Love what you were, how to Love through discomfort and confusion, and how to Love the unknown. Stay open. You're on your way home.

Leave a Lot Up to Mystery

I've been blessed to work with some highly gifted seers and healers in my life. Women and men who could scan you with their inner eye and tell you why your heart was broken and exactly which of your organs needed what minerals. A high-level astrologer should be able to foretell major transitions in your life. Interstellar sages have walked the Earth and prophesied much of what's unfolding in the world this century. But no one—absolutely no one—can determine your future for you.

If you're on a trajectory, we can use logic to guess where you might be headed. Both natural-born talent and paths of destruction are easy to spot.

But the heart always leaves room for miracles, uprisings of group determination, and divine intervention. So rest in mystery. In fact, leverage it to allow yourself to change for the better every single day.

Can't know, don't know, won't know, probably have never known, may never know. But here you are.

Trying to figure out the workings of the Universe while your life is crashing down is going to be crazy-making. Respond to what's right in front of you with all the Love and curiosity that you can, and you'll get what life is trying to teach you. Whether it's a transcendental experience or a baby that needs your attention, nothing is more grand or sacred than what's happening right now.

See the Pain but Don't Stare at It

Some of us put blinders on to our pain. Ignore it, soldier on. Some of us can't take our eyes off it. We spend so much energy therapizing and "working with it" that the hurt can become this whole character in our life. "The thing that happened" comes with us to our new relationships, and it keeps showing up in our social media posts, and every time we talk about or think about our future, there's "the thing that happened" distracting us from what's possible.

There's so much healing to come from disclosure and having our woundedness witnessed. We bring our shadow into the Light through the vessel of relationships. It's the gift of being on a planet with billions of humans—we get to hear and be heard. And . . . but . . .

There comes a time, and it's usually sooner than we'd like to admit, that we need to stop telling the pain story over again. This isn't to minimize the impact of trauma or a tough event, it's so we can heal. Stop giving it more energy. Every time we talk about the same painful event . . . in the same way . . . especially if it's in commiseration, we're feeding our subconscious the same vibration—little paper cuts of "that happened."

I'm not suggesting that we never talk about our past again. (Though that's not an entirely bad idea.) But what if . . .

We only speak about our pain with the intention to heal it. We bring a sacredness to the accounting. We regard the sharing of our pain as an important event. We can be poetic and measured about it, or be an incoherent, hot mess. It doesn't matter what we say, it's how we approach it, and it's who we're approaching it with. If we're mindful in this way, then we're not going to mindlessly keep telling the same story. When we respect our sorrow upfront, more fully, then we'll be less inclined to keep pulling it out later for sympathy. Love it sooner and you can heal sooner.

And then . . . the next time we share about it, we try to tell the story in a different way. And when we talk about the next time, maybe we can share fewer details. And perhaps we can pull back on the amount of people we share the pain story with. And eventually we won't be talking about it much at all. And in direct proportion to that, the pain memory stops looping in our minds.

This is hard work. The ego-mind Loves a good replay and kvetch. It takes a lot of Love to be in Loving silence when our woundedness wants to get attention. But that's exactly the move that adds to the festering. The best medicine is rest. Rest the story, rest the mind, and rest in Love.

Aim for Transmutation

Shed yourself of all that's not aligned with the Truth of you—the money, the identity, the dreams, the reputation, the status. And if all goes to Divine Plan, you might be unrecognizable on the other side of the fire, as every phoenix is.

Change is not a passive event. We really need to understand that "time" doesn't change anything. *Consciousness* does.

Vows lay the map to the future. Dedication creates the future.

We must make the vow to a beautiful ideal, the virtues of the heart, and devote our lives to it. Like we do at births, and weddings, and on deathbeds: we stand in Love, we look ahead, and we promise to make good on the vision.

As structures crumble and so many people are awakening, this is a vividly sacred time to avow a new way of life. We have to come into ceremony with our personal and global suffering. We have to approach it as a passage to higher consciousness, submit our fears, and vow to Love. The ceremony is underway.

Really Letting Go

"How do you let go of attachments to things? Don't even try. It's impossible. Attachment to things drops away by itself when you no longer seek to find yourself in them."
—Eckhart Tolle

We can't let go of anything.

Try right now to let go of a particular fear. You see it in your mind's eye, your thinking wraps around it and . . . Can you let go of it by putting your attention on it? Nope. What we put our attention on grows. Energy follows thought.

And . . . whatever has been brought into existence—whether that's a thoughtform or a sandcastle—doesn't go away by simply excommunicating it in our heads. That's called repression or magical thinking.

You can banish a criminal to the badlands, but the criminal is still in the world. Ideally, the criminal is rehabilitated, healed, so that they're no longer a threat/energy that needs to be exiled.

In this same way, we work with the content that we want to be rid of, and we befriend it. Otherwise, it just comes creeping back and causing trouble. There are no enemies in the heart space—just some fragmented parts of ourselves that we need to keep a loving eye on.

We can't let go of anything.

But we can transform everything.

How do we transform something so that it no longer takes up energy within us?

We LOVE it.

Or we OFFER it up—which is also an act of Love.

When we bring anything into our heart space, it enters into a healing environment where it can be at rest, it can transmute, or it can expand upon its True Nature. The heart is a holistic hospital.

When we welcome in, say, fear to the environment of Love, it begins to relax; it may shift into the energy of care and then grow into Wisdom. (Fear is sometimes just a shadow expression of caring.)

Love helps everything return to its highest expression.

Rather than trying to send our fear packing, we can embrace it. And it will dissolve. And that's the "letting go" that we typically experience, or want to experience.

The heart-as-hospital approach works well for letting go of relationships. Let's say a relationship has come to an end and we're having trouble getting over the pain. We're "focused on letting it go" (we can now see how impossible that is), but because we're focused on letting go instead of healing, we can't let go.

So we turn our attention to healing what it is that we want to let go of. Rather than trying to exile the painful association—whether it's our grief over the ending or we're having to process the damage that may have occurred—we work to heal the energetic dynamic of the relationship.

Every relationship is a container of energy. We can help the container to morph into a new shape. That shape can look like distance or amicable-relating or a new agreement that we haven't yet considered.

Maybe you need to cry for a long time about your losses. Do it. And sure, maybe it's wise to block your ex's phone number. We part ways, we move on, we go to our next assignments in life. We can hold it all with Love, and we allow the situation to shift into a healthier, higher vibration—whatever that looks like.

LOVE LIGHT POWER

Divine Love
is the will to do good for ALL.
It's the ultimate inclusiveness.

Divine Light
is the application of Divine Love.
This means that when we give Love,
it becomes Light. Love given is Light.
We ARE Love, and we point that substance
in a particular direction—to another person,
to a part of ourselves, to a wound or a situation
or to the planet. We're streaming
consciousness, Light, outward.

Divine Power
is inclusiveness and surrender in action.
It's a "Thy will be done" approach to life,
rather than "My will be done."
We trust the unfolding guidance of Spirit,
and we wrap that Love and Light around the world.

@DANIELLELAPORTE

meditate

pray

contemplate

nourish

move

breathe

still

silence

rest

sleep

nature

give thanks

Chapter 28

TOOLS FOR HEART CENTERING

**We're all on our way to finding out
that we're already enlightened.**

SPIRITUAL PRACTICE IS FOR CONNECTING to the Divine and cleansing and healing our energy bodies. And the more we connect with the Divine, the more healing occurs. The more we cleanse—our psyche, our body temples—the more Light makes its way into us.

Ultimately, our spiritual practice is for becoming more Loving. With the meditation, prayers, studies . . . we're not trying to earn our way into heaven or please spiritual authorities. Our dedication serves to *soften us*.

MEDITATE

"If you don't meet yourself on a consistent basis in meditation,
   you're living with a stranger."
   –Guru Singh

"If we want to save the world, we need a plan.
   But no plan will work unless we meditate."
   –His Holiness the 14th Dalai Lama

When someone says they're not "into" committed relationships, I usually think, *Oh ya . . . wait 'til you meet a person whom you actually want to be committed to.* I apply this logic to people's relationship with meditation. If you haven't found a meditation that fits for you yet, keep looking. And just like discovering a right relationship, finding the right meditation can be life-changing.

I hear from meditation-resistant folks things like, "My time on the tread-mill is my meditation." Ohhhkay. Sure, maybe you're tapping the Universal Mind while you're working your glutes. That's entirely possible. But, babe, that's probably not meditation, that's a workout. And dig this: having a more intimate relationship with your heart and mind is going to improve your body connection.

Lots of folks say they fall asleep when they try to meditate. That's all right. You just probably need more sleep. And you can find a meditation that helps you stay awake.

Meditate with no expectations. We don't practice to make something new happen. We meditate to see what's already happening—without judgment.

Questions for many levels of meditators:

What do you want from a meditation practice? Which teachers do you resonate with? Do you want more emphasis on breathwork or visualization? Do you want to be in motion? Are you wanting to chant? Do you want to be guided?

Do you want your practice to be an overt form of seva (selfless service)? Do you want to calm your nervous system or heal relationships? Are you looking to cleanse your mind or land into your heart? Do you want to get into alignment with your Soul? Are you seeking comfort? Guidance? Is this a way to express your gratitude and reverence to Creation?

Meditation isn't one-size-fits-all, and it's helpful to dance with different methods. On the way to finding what works for you, you may feel like a mentally challenged monkey trying to focus for 30 seconds on the Divine while being interrupted by your to-do lists and fantasies. That's okay. That means you're doing it. Keep listening. Keep breathing and letting go.

We're all on our way to finding out that we're already enlightened.

PRAY

> "Despite what Christians have often been taught, prayer is not a technique for getting things, a pious exercise that somehow makes God happy, or a requirement for entry into heaven. It is much more like practicing heaven now by leaping into communion with what is right in front of us."
> –Father Richard Rohr

We pray to heal. To have. We pray for people we Love and for people we have a hard time liking. We sit in prayer circles petitioning for rain and for someone's cancer to dissolve. We can dance prayers or sing them. You can pray in reverence, in shock, in exquisite thanks.

Prayer should be the most ongoingly intimate conversation that we're having in our lives.

For so long, my prayers were a negotiation. I thought that if I gave the Divine my strongest, most diligently believing self, I'd earn what I was asking for. So, I brought my best "I got this" attitude to the Universe—perfectly in order for our "be your best" culture. A Perfectly Devoted Daughter of Life.

Relate?

But what of the days when we are not even close to our best? When we are feeling broken or put upon? When we're short on Faith and long on craving? If we don't reveal our shadow to the Light, where can we go to be healed?

Many saints speak of vulnerability in prayer—a spiritual nakedness in which you disrobe from pretenses and **come to God as you are**. "Disrobing" is a misleading term, as if you slip off your towel for a dip on a sunny day. Soul exposure is usually more of a burning. To the bone. It's very, very *thorough*.

Personally, I thought I was being sufficiently vulnerable. I was peeling it off in therapy. I was mostly certainly telling God about my fears. But what I was not telling God was that, truthfully, I was afraid of my fear . . . and ashamed of my shame . . . and felt terrorized by what terrified me. But that's what I most needed to say.

Our prayer life can include fervent praise. And deep searching. And on some days, the most vulnerable requests: *Take my fear. And take my fear of my fear. Take my shame. Take my shame of my shame. Take my terror. Take my terror of my terror.*

Like great conversations, great prayer is completely honest, very vulnerable, and it works best when we listen deeply.

CONTEMPLATE

> "Contemplation is an alternative consciousness that refuses to identify with or feed what are only passing shows. It is the absolute opposite of addiction, consumerism or any egoic consciousness."
> –Father Richard Rohr

Contemplation is a subtle practice done from the heart. It's not the same as analyzing a subject. You're not tracking an idea or trying to nail down a solution. **Contemplation is when you offer a concept up to your heart for the**

Truth of it to be revealed. Park a topic or idea in your heart and spend some time getting to really know it. Take your time. You're asking your Soul to elucidate.

So, for instance, I wanted to know about the essence of Courage. So I decided to *contemplate* courage for a few months. In the meditation I was doing, I'd place Courage in my heart center as a "virtue seed" and let it blossom. The visual helped anchor my awareness to the energy of courage.

Some days I'd actively try to sense the qualities of Courage, and my heart always had something to show me, in its wordless but articulate way. Other times, I'd go for a walk and just have a conversation with courage. Not surprisingly, insights and inspirational material started showing up in my life. And Courage began to feel very friendly and known to me. (What I saw was that its central energy is not about "boldness": it's about *presence*. The Courage to really be with whatever is happening.)

Choose a virtue or a high-frequency energy to contemplate . . . Openness. Unity. Harmlessness. Gentleness. Happiness. Miracles. Devotion . . .

Close your eyes and just reflect. You can try it now. And maybe you can keep reflecting on a particular virtue or high-vibe quality for a few weeks or months. Walk around the block with it, bring the word to your morning prayer. Take a bath with it. And then watch how, say, Generosity or Loving Kindness begin to present themselves inside of and around you. The Universe always answers our committed curiosity.

NOURISH

> "Treat yourself as if you already are enough. Walk as if you are enough. Eat
> as if you are enough. See, look, listen as if you are enough. Because it's true."
> –Geneen Roth

REFLECTION. What's your common language or terms around food and eating?

What's your curiosity level around where your food comes from, how and who produced or packaged it?

Do you have a gratitude practice around meals? What might that look like for you?

MOVE

> "If you want to give birth to your true self, you are going to have
> to dig deep down into that body of yours and let your Soul howl.
> Sometimes you have to take a leap of faith and trust that if you turn
> off your head, your feet will take you where you need to go."
> –Gabrielle Roth

The body's function is to transmit Love.

My beautiful friend Rochelle Schieck created a movement system called Qoya. She always says, "Through movement, we remember." We're remembering our connection to Source.

Beyond fitness and building physical strength, how can you move to experience your body as a conductor of Love? Could be dance, yoga, an ocean swim, nursing, jumping jacks, handholding, healing touch . . .

If we intend to use our bodies as vehicles of learning, then we're going to be shown the deeper essence of who we are.

BREATHE

> "Every breath contains the possibility of transformation
> from a contracted state to something more elegant."
> –Scott Schwenk

I used to think breathwork was too "lite." Like, how could it be more effective than crying in a workshop full of strangers or doing a coffee colonic? I was grossly underestimating my respiratory system.

Breath brings us to our most primal and profound power. Mindful breathing is the surest way to come into the present moment and tap into our innate trust in life.

And! It cleanses toxic build-up in the body, nourishes our nervous system, and helps us process emotions.

If we ever need evidence that we are held by life, we only need to inhale. When I'm feeling any degree of *woe is me* or that I have to do *everything myself*, I take a deep breath and remember that something greater than me is always, no matter what, breathing me. When I sleep. Right now. Always. Life is constantly supporting me.

Our breath and awareness of our breath are powerful allies through these times. They're the Spirit that connects us all.

Source is always breathing us. It's holding us through our contractions and our expansions. And when we turn our attention to that life force, we will only ever find healing.

PRACTICE
Left Nostril Breathing

(ALSO KNOWN AS CHANDRA ANGA PRANAYAMA)

When intense emotions pass through, use this exercise to come back to the breath. Align with the cyclical patterns of each inhale and exhale, and you'll calm your nervous system.

Left nostril breathing activates and stabilizes the parasympathetic system. This is a simple, powerful breathing technique for calming the nervous system. The calmer our nervous system is, the healthier our immune function.

Do this any time. All the time. It's especially great when you wake up and go to bed.

You'll be breathing in and out through your left nostril and can use different breath ratios to emphasize different benefits of the practice.

Use a ratio of 1:1 (equal inhale and exhale) to steady yourself.

Use a ratio of 1:2 (exhale is double the length of the inhale) to deeply calm and relax.

1. Use your right thumb to plug your right nostril. Keep the fingers on your right hand extended, like little antennas pointing upward.

2. Inhale through your left nostril—deeply and fully. Fill your belly and lungs.

3. Exhale through your left nostril—deeply and fully. Empty your belly and lungs.

4. Start with seven rounds (one round = inhale + exhale). Once you feel comfortable there, work your way up and repeat for as many cycles as you like, or until you feel calmer and more grounded.

STILL

"Much of spiritual work is slowing down enough to
let our minds come into harmony with our hearts."

–Ram Dass

Our hearts ache for stillness. In our productivity-obsessed societies, stillness is a revolution. Do you long for it? Or does the very concept of stillness
make you panicky? The absence of distraction can make us feel vulnerable,
exposed to the whims of our emotions, which is why you might long for
stillness AND be panicky at the thought of it. Don't be. Getting there is not
as tough as you might think.

Tapping the power of stillness is about *sequencing*. It's not about how much
stillness you can create in your day. It's about *when* you create it.

You might want to try **a stillness sandwich. It's like this: be still in the
beginning, rock 'n' roll in the middle, and be still at the end.**

At the beginning of any endeavor—a project, a relationship, a new day (this
is why mornings are so sacred)—be in stillness so you can access a flow
state. Stop long enough to hear your Soul give you directions. Then go, go,
go, if that's what's called for.

Then, toward the end (of the day, project, relationship), wrap with active
stillness. This is how we transfer our experience into Wisdom.

It's really the same principle of savasana, the final "corpse" pose of most
yoga classes. One of my favorite Canadian yogis, Eoin Finn, has a sweet
anecdote about how doing yoga without completing savasana at the end is
like mixing the ingredients for a cake and then neglecting to bake it: all the
ingredients are there, but it's not yet a cake until it's baked. We become still
to integrate the benefits of all the work we've done.

Stillness isn't the absence of movement. It's a focus on the present. And it's the only way that we can process our learning into Wisdom.

SILENCE

> "Silence is not an absence of sound but rather a shifting of
> attention toward sounds that speak to the Soul."
>
> –Thomas Moore

Unfolding. Agitation. Crunchy. Relishing. Golden. Home. Safety. Expansiveness. Awakening.

What's your relationship to silence? Do you seek it? Avoid it? When was the last time you intentionally chose silent time? Does the thought of three days in a cabin without music or TV make you anxious . . . or longing?

What's the quality of silence between you and other people? Do you fill the air with sounds?

What does listening feel like? Can you support yourself to listen more? Or more Lovingly? And that includes listening to yourself. With kindness. Compassion. Gentle curiosity.

In silence, a broken heart is reminded that it is alone . . . and held. An overbusy mind is challenged by peace . . . and given space to unfurl. Silence is where we can go to know what wants to be known.

REST

> "You will not be left behind if you pause. You will gain more
> insight about your journey. This may cause you to change
> course. Perhaps that is what some fear in the pause? That
> they will finally realize another way is calling them."
>
> –Octavia Raheem

Want to know the most life-enhancing spiritual counsel that I've ever been given in all my life, by one of the most powerful energy healers I've ever known? This is it:

Take breaks.

That's it. Take breaks. We go farther that way, and we're alive when we get to where we're going.

•

You've done a lot of good, hard work. You're full, fatigued, ever-committed.

Do you want to go even farther? To be more effective, Radiant, powerful?

Then rest.

Rest because you need it. (Notice I didn't say "deserve it." Rest is not something we need to earn.) Rest because you Love—yourself, your body, your mind, the world. Rest because there is always more beautiful work to be done. Rest to become stronger. Rest to become wiser.

Rest is Love.

What does it say about our culture that resting can be a difficult feat? It says we are steered by capitalism, toxic patriarchy, and the mortal coil of self-worth issues. We know this.

So let me try to convince you how rest will move you forward. (This is a mind trick, I'm appealing to our obsession with productivity. My plan is to get you to rest for performance-enhancement reasons, and then it's going to touch your spirit and you'll be like, *Rest is Love, and Love is all, and that is that!*)

There is an uncomfortable—and sacred—space between exertion and restoration. If we skip over it, we'll miss the insights of all the work we have done—insights that will guide us to the next step. **If we don't rest, we won't see what we learned along the way.** If we don't learn from what we've just done, we're going to repeat bad habits and eclipse healthy impulses that we should be building on.

Rest to become stronger.

Rest to become wiser.

Rest is Love.

SLEEP

> "The best bridge between despair and
>   hope is a good night's sleep."
>
>   –E. Joseph Cossman

Here's a very simple, beautiful practice for restorative sleep from *Radiant Rest* by Tracee Stanley:

> "Tonight, as you go to sleep place a prayer, a blessing, a bible verse,
>   or mantra in the heart as you drift off to sleep.
>
> As you wake up spend some time freewriting and spend time
>   meditating or practicing yoga nidra.* Open yourself to your
>   inner wisdom."

When we practice yoga nidra, we not only experience the power of deep rest and relaxation, but we get to wake up to our essential nature, one that is filled with Radiance and bliss. This awakening has lasting transformative effects on every aspect of our lives.

*Yoga nidra (Sanskrit), or "yogic sleep," is a state of consciousness between waking and sleeping, like the "going-to-sleep" stage, typically induced by a guided meditation.

NATURE

"We do not 'come into' this world; we come out of it, as leaves from a tree. As the ocean 'waves,' the universe 'peoples.' Every individual is an expression of the whole realm of nature, a unique action of the total universe."

–Alan Watts

"All nature will commune with you when you are in tune with God. Realization of this truth will make you master of your destiny."

–Paramahansa Yogananda

Everything we have, everything we are, is because of Mother Earth. Our buildings are made of her body. Our vehicles, our technologies, our cures . . . all made of her body. We are from and of her. Every relationship we have . . . her. We owe Mother Earth ALL.

Take your praise and your pain and offer it all to Gaia. Praise her for pulsing through you and all sentient beings.

And when we offer up our pain, it's not to dump our toxicity on her—she's had enough of that. But instead, we can place it on her like we would put a candle on our altar. *Here, this is sacred. Thank you.*

Nature is the connection to the Divine Feminine. The Earth is like a battery charger of energy. Ideally, we enter into a conscious relationship with nature with sacred intention—for communion and homage. The intention deepens our restoration.

Be outside often.

Sit or stand with your spine against a tree.

Walk barefoot on the ground.

Swim in lakes and salt water—it's one of the greatest energy cleansers.

Breathe in the cold.

Bask in the sun.

Praise her Generosity and Resilience.

Be aware of the Earth's presence in all you do.

GIVE THANKS

"When you go deeply into the present, gratitude arises
spontaneously, even if it's just gratitude for breathing, gratitude
for the aliveness that you feel in your body. Gratitude is there
when you acknowledge the aliveness of the present moment."

–Eckhart Tolle

Gratitude is a quality of the heart . . . that's good for our brain chemistry (as all qualities of the heart are).

University of California–Davis studied people who kept a weekly gratitude list compared to people who kept a list of things that irritated them. And whaddya know? They concluded that "a conscious focus on blessings may have emotional and interpersonal benefits."

We know this.

Gratitude stimulates the brain's hypothalamus, which regulates stress. It also tickles the area called the ventral tegmental, which produces feelings of pleasure. So, we can conclude: appreciation is a form of wellness.

Gratitude is the most immediate route to your inner strength.

And it's generative: gratitude attracts more reasons to be grateful.

Gratitude interrupts anxiety and anger. It's a high-vibration coping tool.

How do you get animosity, hostility, anger, and fear out of your heart? Gratitude, gratitude. The vibration of gratitude is a solvent for low-frequency emotions. In those moments of duress, an argument, or abandonment, you might only be able to access the most basic appreciation. But reach for anything. *I'm grateful for good teeth. I'm thankful for food in my fridge.* And then keep aiming higher until you land on appreciation for the nature of impermanence and, oh, I don't know, maybe the awe of eternity? All in good time.

Our Heart Centered Leaders take people through an exercise where they write Love letters to their positive *and* negative feelings and then they look at what there is to be grateful for. We cover the spectrum. What's amazing is that when people see what's to be grateful for in their suffering, it changes the way they see their suffering *and* themselves.

And really, isn't it so much better to be in a state of gratitude than misery? Being thankful doesn't preclude feeling suffering. Pain is pain, hurt is hurt. We honor that. But when we simultaneously choose gratitude, we raise the energy for everyone. Gratitude uplifts everything.

PRACTICE
The Metta Bhavana Prayer

May I be happy.

May I be healthy.

May I be free of suffering.

May I be free of mental anxiety.

May I live in peace.

May my life be blessed with ease.

May you be happy.

May you be healthy.

May you be free of suffering.

May you be free of mental anxiety.

May you live in peace.

May your life be blessed with ease.

May we be happy.

May we be healthy.

May we be free of suffering.

May we be free of mental anxiety.

May we live in peace.

May our lives be blessed with ease.

Translated from Pali (the original language of most Buddhist prayer and teaching). Metta means "Loving Kindness;" Bhavana means "cultivation." Legend says that after listening to monks' complaints about their experience retreating to the forest, the Buddha gave them the Metta Bhavana Prayer and instructed them to go back into the woods and practice relentlessly. It's said that the monks re-emerged enlightened.

Chapter 29

RECEPTIVITY

Receptivity is empowerment.

HISTORICALLY, WE'VE BEEN TRAINED to think of power as forceful-ness or dominance. Power over. Power through. Power player.

In an enlightened world, **receptivity** is the real "power."

Real power can only be generated from a pure source. Source itself is incor-ruptible. Why take direction from corrupted systems and poisoned pools of knowledge when you can go straight to the Divine for guidance?

Your Soul is waiting patiently for you to ask for guidance. The scripts from our past won't help in charting the future. Our ego-mind is going to exhaust us with chasing goals and deliverables.

All that Creation asks of us is to be receptive and willing to listen.

REFLECTION. Let's tap into the energy of basking. Basking is such a gorgeous idea: "To relax in a pleasant warmth or atmosphere." See your-self on a beautiful beach or in a field, lying under glorious sunlight. And you're just basking. Nothing to do but bask. You don't have to think about it. You don't have to be excellent at it. There's no basking competition to win. You're just entirely open to receiving all the nourishment that the sunlight is shining down directly on to you.

What if creative power worked the same way? We just bask in the Light of our Soul? We simply receive and follow higher guidance.

If receptivity to the Divine is what true power is, then creating conditions of relaxation becomes the most viable means of empowerment. Since we're more receptive when we're calm. Maybe we're honor bound to just . . . *relax.*

I think this is what the sages mean when they tell us that *there is nowhere to go and nothing to do.* Just relax. And listen.

Experience yourself under the Light of Creation and let it heal and guide you. You don't need a book or an app to tell you where to go. You don't need to train for this or be there on time. You just need to be willing to honor the pace of the heart and receive what's always already been there for you: endless Higher Guidance.

You don't need to push for the answer. It will come. You don't need to be ahead of the curve or to finish in first place. Receptivity doesn't need to compete or scramble.

Real power tunes inward. It chooses to expand, to blossom on its own time, to wait. It shares its power with others. It's not force . . . it's flow.

> "Love is the real power. It's the energy that cherishes. The more you work with that energy, the more you will see how people respond naturally to it, and the more you will want to use it. It brings out your creativity, and helps everyone around you flower. Your children, the people you work with—everyone blooms."
> –Marion Woodman

When we say that we're going to "go with the flow," what we're really declaring is that we're going to step into the creative principle of life—we're going to be receptive to divine guidance, in the middle of the river: in the flow.

When you're going with the flow, you are collaborating with life, you're allowing for all the healing that is available and always being offered to you to be assimilated into your being.

Going with the flow is dynamic, not passive. We receive, we respond. We receive, we respond.

Receptivity is about alert relaxation. You're relaxed, you're flexible, and you're paying very close attention. It is a wide-awake trust.

Receptivity to the Divine is counterculture, of course. It doesn't rely on mood-altering substances or anyone else's authority. If we all look to Love for the answers, there's no quick fix or dogma to sell us.

●

Some of my Sufi friends, a wife and husband, told me they'd both come to a point on their spiritual path where they'd stopped asking for anything from a Higher Power. No more praying, no more petitioning. They were devout practitioners. They'd authored multiple prayer books. And I was this go-make-it-happen Gen-Xer recovering Catholic. So this was a wild concept for me.

"You just . . . don't ask for anything anymore?" I tried to clarify.

"Nope, it's all handled," she answered.

"So, wait . . . you don't turn to God for things. You . . . don't even pray?"

"Well, you can pray, but it's more about listening," he said.

There was a lot of vodka that night. So a bit baffled and buzzed, I had to further clarify.

"So you just . . . *receive*?" I queried.

They were so patient with me.

"Well, what else can you do, Danielle?" they both smiled.

And honestly, I thought to myself, *Well you can hustle your ass off and keep praying. I for one am going to keep praying!*

But we all raised a glass to receptivity.

And eventually, thanks to the infinite patience of the Divine, I learned the power of basking in Soul Light. It's much better for me than being ambitious.

Receptivity is our most empowered way of being. But it can be a terrifying proposition to a personality that's been working overtime for decades. Relaxation and receptivity are channels that we learn how to fine tune. More reflection gets us better reception.

When we turn the channel to *Thy will be done*, we become receptors for Love. That's attunement. And that's real power.

Chapter 30

UNIFY

A thesis on Love in these times:

We need to heal.

We need each other.

We need each other to heal.

And that's that.

To Heal the World, Heal Yourself

We're conditioned to believe that we have to work to fix everything outside of us to make life more workable. What if that's just another fabrication of the ego personality?

Because what often happens in our activism and best intentions to repair people and save the world is a lot of blaming and shaming. We waste heaps of energy policing other people's behavior. But the Higher Self has a message: check *yourself*.

> "Correcting oneself is correcting the whole world. The sun is simply bright. It does not correct anyone. Because it shines, the whole world is full of light. Transforming yourself is a means of giving light to the whole world."
> –Ramana Maharshi

How does this perspective sit with those of us who are fired up about all things political that are so very personal? What about social responsibility?

What about being change agents? What about fighting for peace? Fighting . . . for . . . peace.

We can't fight for peace. The journey has to reflect the intended destination.

And we can't fight "against another" because that "other" is ourselves. And "their" actions are reflections of our inner state. The outer world—what mystics call a dream state—is a reflection of our inner world.

The socially responsible path is to heal ourselves of whatever is raging within us. To become un-triggerable. Steady in all storms. Loving everyone and all that arises.

Imagine if you and I and our neighbors and colleagues and all the teachers and CEOs and parents and prime ministers and everyone everywhere worked on healing our very own selves. It would be Love anarchy! Wars would end, and cults would collapse. Big Pharma would go bankrupt. Advertising agencies would be having bake sales.

World peace starts with self-actualization.

●

The unhealed self wants to "save the world" out of a sense of guilt and striving to be good. It sees service as a means to feeling accepted and more worthy. This is the shadowy territory where virtue can flip into vice.

We can volunteer at a soup kitchen because we think it will earn us divine favor with God or good PR. Or . . . we can volunteer at a soup kitchen because we feel connected to humanity. *That's my brother, these children could be mine, that could be me, this is us.*

The small self wants to save the world to feel bigger. Shadow "service." The heart wants to heal the world because it needs healing. Soul service.

When we apply Compassion to ourselves, that Love will naturally flower outward. And we'll serve from a place of fullness, not despair. This is one of the most stunning cycles of personal growth: **when we see our inner Light, it shows us that we're all connected**. And then everything we do is on behalf of our relatedness and shared impact.

> "The New Story is actually the ancient story. The New Story is the story of reunion and inter-being. You are not separate. Who you are is a nexus of relationships, and actions of Love counter the story of separation."
> –Charles Eisenstein

Harmlessness

> "Love is creative and redemptive. Love builds up and unites; hate tears down and destroys. The aftermath of the 'fight with fire' method which you suggest is bitterness and chaos. The aftermath of the Love method is reconciliation and creation of the beloved community. Physical force can repress, restrain, coerce, destroy, but it cannot create anything organized, only Love can do that. Yes, Love—which means understanding, creativity, redemptive goodwill, even for one's enemies—is the solution to the race problem."
> –Martin Luther King Jr.

There's a warriorship to Love, to Light work. Ask the sacred land protectors, the suffragettes, or anybody who Loves a child.

But we have to fight for what is right without the intention to cause harm. We have to be mindful that in the *rebalancing* between Love and ignorance that we don't become what we're opposing—that we don't divide with our words, actions, dollars, or hashtags.

Most movies have an antagonist. The bad guy plays a crucial role in every story. He agitates change; he starts the fire that initiates the hero. Where there's darkness, there will be Light.

When the movie's over, we all understand that the guy who played the villain is very likely a good dude in real life. He's an actor doing his job; he goes home when it's a wrap.

What if it's similar in the planetary drama that we call "real life"? We're all Souls, playing our Earth roles. And when we're done here, we go back to our genuine Divine Nature. Some of us incarnate to stir up shit . . . that creates the compost . . . that helps humanity flourish.

Everyone is playing their part in the great unfolding that's happening on Earth. The oppressors and the freedom fighters. The mad and the sane. The cancellers and the meditators. The silent and the outspoken.

We can strive to right the social wrongs without condemning the individuals to hell. They will deal with their own karma, you don't need to add to yours by stirring up hate on the way to justice. Put your energy on the ideal outcome, not on tearing down the bad actors.

We rarely know what's going on behind the interdimensional curtain. What often looks like a tragedy can be a work of art in the making.

Manifest Love

The days of self-centered bucket lists are over. This era is calling for heart centered visions.

What if next to photos of dream homes and hot bods on our vision boards, we also glued on images of lush forests and happy neighbors? Maybe our monthly goals incorporated a prayer practice for everyone in recovery.

Focus on the energy of the solution.

What if corporate growth objectives put their community contribution spending on par with shareholders' profit?

Heart centered manifesting principles:

- Our outer world desires—to do, to have, to be, to experience— take into consideration the potential benefit or harm to others and the planet.
- Our visions for our own happiness, wellness, and prosperity include others' happiness, wellness, and prosperity.
- We ask: Who can I include? Who can I welcome? Who can I lift up?
- We ask: How can we ease each other's pain?
- We ask: How can I use my fulfillment to benefit others?

Serve with Joy

"For as long as space endures,
And for as long as living beings remain,
Until then may I, too, abide
To dispel the misery of the world."

    –Shantideva

All the fulfillment we seek can be found in service to others. Service can take multitudinous forms. We can focus on cleaning up our energy field or our local beach. We can nurse, or we can teach. We can run assembly lines or marathons. We could wait tables. We could await the will of heaven in a cloister. A hermit or a socialite.

The form of our lives doesn't matter as much as the spirit that guides our choices. We're either vivifying Love or just killing time.

How do we serve in these challenging times? How do you make a contribution as your heart is breaking open and the whole world is getting a wake-up call? I think the answer is in our joy.

Your joy is your service to the collective.

And your service is where you'll find your joy.

Do what comes most naturally to you. There's a beautiful Hindu concept called swadharma (swa, "own," + dharma, "duty"): "the lawful conduct of oneself based on one's ability." The idea is that if we're aligned with our True Nature, our actions become more effortless. Less pretense makes for more glide. We speak and act from our hearts. And we avoid attempting to walk anyone else's path. Using our unique sensibilities in service to others is the richness of our life.

How to serve with joy? Simple: Be yourself and help out.

•

HOW MAY I SERVE?

Root so deeply into your heart that comparison and materialism, and status quo idealism, and the lie called media realism cannot possibly sway your Truth.

Don't chase for motivation. Be a devotee of inspiration.

Do what ambition tells you not to do. Forget your goals and regimens. Be very still and listen to the pain of our world. Then it will be very clear what to do.

You will let your sacred heart blaze to find solutions fierce with Love. You will hold the babies and kiss the ground and share seeds.

You will rest and regroup.

You'll reach out and you will deeply listen. You will remember why we fell in Love in the first place.

Everywhere you go, you will bring your joy to bear on the situation. Because, as you know, we all walk on common ground.

And that is the joy of your service
and the service of your joy.

My heart is your heart is our heart.

Chapter 31

FOCUS FORWARD

Always be seeing the beauty.

Sweeping with Light

Begin to focus on the beauty of any situation and you know what will happen? Some ugliness and chaos are going to show up for your attention—like moths to a Soul flame. Relax into peace and you know what you can expect? The mind noise will get more shrill. When you commit to continuously choosing joy, yep . . . old sorrows will surface.

The swing between higher states of being and old memories is a cycle of purification. This is how thorough progress happens. That pendulum of awareness sweeps between our luminosity and our density. We are being trained to become more steady in our heart. It can be wearisome, for sure. But eventually, we'll have swept out enough closeted skeletons and energy blocks that we'll find some calm. In this cleaner space, the reactivity of the subconscious won't be as extreme—there's less sweeping and weeping, and more inner peace.

> **When we open ourselves to Higher Guidance,**
>
> **the Light shows us what needs**
>
> **more Love and care.**

And as we do the Loving,

we begin to stabilize in

a higher vibration.

As I deepened in heart centered practices, I was shocked by what started to surface in my being. Boatloads of fear. I'd always thought of myself as a brave person. Bold, even. But as I surrendered my life more to God, intense fears of trial and tribulation presented themselves.

Would I be asked to sacrifice everything? Would suffering be my qualification for peace? Was I avoiding suffering or delaying joy? Was avoiding suffering going to compound suffering? Was this all a test to choose peace? The more I prayed to have my fears removed, the more fears lined up to be blessed.

This was the revelation that there was a battle going on within me. This process went on for a few years. But it marked the ending of a lifelong held misperception that the Holy existed outside of my human self. Of course, nothing could be further from the Truth.

I was meditating, studying, actively looking for—and finding—the good in everyone. I was becoming more adept at accepting whatever challenge or more obvious blessing was showing up in my body, in my life, in the world. I was feeling so incredibly held by the Infinite. And then, like a flash flood comes in, I'd feel guilty for *existing*. I'd have transcendental experiences of being connected to other people, to trees, to the Great Mother, and then! indescribable fears of annihilation and loneliness would plow through me within moments sometimes.

The heightened states weren't manic. I was making very real, irreversible progress toward my truer nature. But with every move toward oneness awareness, another demon that I'd been trying to cast out showed up for severance pay. They appeared in the form of fear, a toxic thought, or a painful physical flare-up. Eventually, like a good mother would do, I invited all of those outcasts to come inside. They were my creations, after all. I made them; I would take them back, kindly.

And with that steady caring, the battle steadily came to an end.

Loving Kindness is (r)evolutionary.

The Upside of Denial

The only good use of denial is to deny the darkness any power over you. When you're overflowing with Loving awareness, you seal off access points to negativity.

We don't ignore the existence of dark energy and oppositional force. We don't act like the world is in balance when it's clearly askew. We see the intruder, and then we choose to focus on what protects us. There's no need to go near the toxic substances. We don't need to engage with them. We just keep moving in the direction of sanity and wellness, and anything that's trying to feed on us will wither away or go elsewhere.

Fear feeds on fear. Darkness wants you scared.

Love wants you to know that you are protected by Love.

I am Love. That's that.

I work for the Light. That's that.

I only take orders from Divine Power. That's that.

On Purpose

How phenomenal would it be to organize our societies and commerce based on the principles of Loving Kindness? It would be phenomenally purposeful.

Wouldn't it be amazing if teens could go to their high school guidance counselor or parents and say, "I want a career that's compassionate," or "I'm aiming for a dynamic future in morality and human connection"? In so many cases, educational systems are set up to promote greed in the guise of helping young adults "fulfill their dreams." If our big dreams were filled with Love-centered strategies, then we wouldn't have to cycle back in our late forties to make a more meaningful life.

Love is your purpose, and your unique offering is your calling.

First, focus on the virtues you want to embody, and then your expression in the world will come into focus. The virtue is the horse that pulls the cart of personal expression.

We can get spun out looking in so many directions for our unique life purpose, for our special dharma, when really our purpose is to express the Love that we are made of.

And that can be expressed in so many ways. As we set our intention to live Compassionately or to radiate Loving Kindness, those energy frequencies will pour into us, and then a more formed expression will begin to take shape. Virtues are the function, your lifestyle is the form.

The Point of Love

Dancers stay balanced by fixing their eyes on a focal point. A steady intention allows for optimal flexibility. In the waves of change, let the Light of your heart be the focal point.

Your heart will notice what we all have in common. Focus on that. Your heart will show you a more beautiful vision of the future. Focus on that. Your heart will show you what to be grateful for. Focus on that.

> **We do not need to focus on "fixing" ourselves.**
>
> **As we focus on living from our heart center—from Love— anything that's not in alignment with that Light will fall away.**

You are not in need of more judgment or faultfinding. Stop looking for reasons that you're less than acceptable. **Focus on celebrating rather than critiquing.** We are all in need of more Loving Kindness. And when that flows, anything that's out of sorts will naturally come into balance.

What we focus on grows.

Focus on Love at all times.

How will you know if what you're focused on is truly aligned with Love or right action? You'll know. And if you get it wrong, you can course-correct and be the wiser for it. It's all grist for grace. But just to be clear . . .

Right action stems from inclusiveness. Right action considers the potential benefit or harm to all beings—ourselves included.

There's no need for martyrdom in your world service. Your happiness and health can benefit the collective. Your prosperity and protection are good for our community.

Here's a simple guiding question to ask yourself and others every day: How can all beings be happy and free?

This fits with Immanuel Kant's moral philosophy: "Act as if the maxims of your action were to become through your will a universal law of nature." That's a bit of pressure. But it's just another take on the Golden Rule: "Do unto others as you would have others do unto you." Which leads us into the unified field of Love, where we understand that the "other" is also "me."

The Beautiful Now

> "It was easy to Love God in all that was beautiful.
>   The lessons of deeper knowledge, though,
>   instructed me to embrace God in all things."
>   –Saint Francis of Assisi

The most common counsel I've been given by great teachers essentially boils down to this:

Leave the past where it is: in the past. A strong mind focuses forward.

Let's raise that even higher.

A strong mind focuses forward by seeing the beauty in the situation.

Always be seeing the beauty.

Allow me again to point to Ephesians 5:13: ". . . everything exposed by the light becomes visible—and everything that is illuminated becomes a light."

When you find the beauty in the ugly, you change the ugly into the beautiful.

This is deep Light work, and it will require diligence. The people or situations that repulse you? Create a Loving thought. *We're all from the same source.* The agony in your body or in your mind . . . Can you find one beautiful aspect of what you're going through? Maybe it's that you're slowing down, or that you're more in touch with your body, or that you're learning how loved you are. Maybe it's just that you're noticing the trees in a way that you never have.

Switch the thought that spots the reason to be upset or repulsed. Focus on the sweet in the bittersweet.

There is always Light in the darkness. Mine for it.

Exalt, glorify, elevate, rejoice.

Exalt the beauty in all. This isn't always straightforward, but it's reliably alchemizing. **When you identify the beautiful in the ugly, what appeared as undesirable is now transformed into something that belongs.** You've realized Love.

And from here, we create a more beautiful future.

Peace

Peace today? Peace in chaos? During the most sweeping upheaval in centuries? Peace when we all seem so polarized? Yes! Yes, of course!

We are here to be the divine counterbalance. **Light warriorship isn't as much about fighting off the "darkness" as it is about focusing on Love while ignorance tries to distract us.**

Peace may not seem as profitable or glamorous as what social gains seem to offer. But as our bucket list starts to leak, the yearning for peace get prioritized.

Please Continue to Heal

Keep giving your most tender self the Love that it's requesting every day. Loving Kindness is the healing methodology that we're all looking for.

If you're inclined, include all sentient beings in your vision for happiness and health—then back it up with action.

Point your requests for guidance to the Highest Sources: to your Soul and the Source that holds your Soul.

If we give up our attachments to timing, then we can trust the inevitability of our healing. And if we stop judging what we've made of ourselves, we'll make better lives, with more Love.

Hopelessness feeds the purveyors of division and doom. Don't go there. Faith is fueled by community. Look into the eyes of the person or the animal next to you with the intention to see their Light—and you'll find it everywhere.

Let's stick together and hold hands every step of the way.

Always with Love,

P.S. Can you see the sky from where you are right now? If not, close your eyes and imagine that stratospheric dome of light blue arching over you. You with me?

I was sitting on a park bench with my man. We were in front of the ocean right after a big rain. It was like the heavens exhaled after a great conversation. The moment lent itself to a philosophical question. And Will pondered, "I wonder how we're really supposed to spend our time in life?"

I think he was asking the sky, but I was preparing my best possible answer.

I thought about all of us tapping our daily plans into an app. Spending time. Taking time. Making time. I thought of the temple monks I heard in India, chanting for the cessation of our suffering, surfing the illusion of time.

Then I wondered, *How would the sky relate to time? If you're limitless, why bother to measure anything?*

So I asked Will, "Can you conceive of being as big as this sky? Like, your True Nature, your heart being *this VAST*?"

His response was characteristically modest. "But I'm just a speck," he said.

"Well, I think you're spectacular," we laughed.

Then we made out. Which was the perfect segue to my best possible answer:

"I think we're all here to figure out how to be Loving," I offered. "You know, just really give 'er."

He agreed.

May we all be so blessed.

We do not need
to focus on
"fixing" ourselves.

As we focus on
living from our heart
center—from Love—
anything that's not in
alignment with that
Light will fall away.

GRATEFUL

With respect to the land and those who have come before me, I acknowledge that I live on the unceded territories of the Musqueam, Squamish, and Tsleil-Waututh First Nations in British Columbia.

Respect for Teachers

In almost every instance in *How to Be Loving*, I quote works and people whose teachings have influenced how I see life. My choice inspirations are:

Adyashanti @adyashanti.ogs | adyashanti.opengatesangha.org

Michael Bernard Beckwith @michaelbbeckwith | michaelbeckwith.com

Cynthia Bourgeault @cynthiabourgeault | cynthiabourgeault.org

Pema Chödrön @anipemachodron | pemachodronfoundation.org

A Course in Miracles | acim.org

Father Richard Rohr @cacradicalgrace | cac.org

Mooji @mooji.official | mooji.org

Eckhart Tolle @eckharttolle | eckharttolle.com

Torkom Saraydarian | tsgfoundation.org

Marianne Williamson @mariannewilliamson | marianne.com

Paramahansa Yogananda @selfrealizationfellowship | yogananda.org

Yoga Sutras of Patanjali

Once in many lifetimes a true healer comes to share the load and help you learn what Divine Love is. For me, that's an energy healer named **V.S.** Her esoteric skill and dedication to unfolding Christ Consciousness have been the most instructional gifts of my life. Her Wisdom is woven into these pages and absolutely everything that I offer. V., I love you like sunrise.

Some of the practices in this book are micro versions of the curriculum for our Heart Centered Leaders Program. Over the course of a year, we had a "bridge team" of seasoned facilitators who helped evolve the program to the depth and reach it has today. I have the most respectful appreciation for: **Alisha Anguiano-Espinoza, Patricia Brannan, Sara Brush, Michele Calderigi, Melanie Clark Pullen, Kellee Ann Dawson, Lisa Duerre, Jacquie Costron, Mackenzie Costron, Tui Fleming, Renee Honrada, Irina Kuligina, Angie Krenz, Mellissa Last, Marisa McAdams, Ann Marie McKenzie, Tricia Millice, Alison Murphy, Claire Nabke, Jackie Nees, Helena Önneby, Monica Paige, Kathryn Sanford, Shawn Marie Turi, Corrie Warrington, and Laura Lee Wood.**

In legion, there are hundreds of **Heart Centered Leaders**, facilitating from many countries, whose reports of "Compassion circles" or workshops on resilience and client conversations, keep me in a state of awe. I always envision you as points of Light on the planet.

There's a beautiful community of seekers that I meet with every other week, in our **Heart Centered Membership**. I'm so grateful to the women (and a few rad men) who show up with deep questioning about healing and serving. So much of that inquiry and group Love inspired *How to Be Loving*, and so many times while writing, I felt like we were in our Heart to Heart calls.

Work with bright, loving people who make you laugh and honor their word and you can't go wrong. Certified Integral Master Coaches **Chela Davison, Nicole Fegely, Holiday Phillips**, and **Andrew Leonard**, with the unfailing support of **Bonnie McRae** helped the Heart Centered Leaders Program become brighter and truly inclusive.

Sounds True is a heart centered publisher, and it's such a blessing to keep growing together. **Tami Simon** has my great respect. And I'm so grateful for the strength and vibrancy of **Jaime Schwalb**. Our content editor **Buzzy Jackson** found me wandering in the woods with an unfinished book and gave me a popcorn trail to coherence. There is a very seasoned team bringing this book to the world—thank you to the copyeditors who put up with my capitalizations of Love and Earth; for **Brian Galvin**'s marketing perspective and the passionate publicity team; and for the vision of **Sibyl Chavis & The Wizards**.

Marcie D read a late edition of this draft and said what I needed to hear in the 11th hour: "It doesn't suck, keep going." **Candis Hoey** has been my salt of the Earth, with a side of cheese, for the longest time. How loving are *we*?! The lovingest. **Annabelle** and **Dennis** have been the gift of all gifts: relatively sane, truly loving parents, who helped me be true to myself.

I am surrounded and supported by women who make their Love visible in our work everyday: the illimitable **Dee Bailey, Katie Gyoffry, Renee Masur**, and **Sarah Miller**. You are each so beautiful and capable. And, Renee, you've held so much of this content with such deep care. What a gift.

All timing is Divine, but like, *I fell in Love* while writing this book. Clearly my Soul wanted to test all my theories, so she sent me **Will**. And purely by example, he showed me how to be even more Loving. My Love, what an honor to be your Love.

And my son . . . **HLJ**. You've taught me one of the greatest virtues of all: patience. And not because I've had to be patient with you. But because you've been so patient with me. Thank you, thank you, thank you.

ABOUT DANIELLE LAPORTE

Danielle LaPorte is the creator of the Heart Centered Membership and the Heart Centered Leaders Program with 400+ facilitators and coaches in 30 countries hosting conversation circles, retreats, and workshops in all kinds of communities and businesses.

She's a member of Oprah's SuperSoul 100 and the former director of a future studies think tank in Washington, DC, where she managed a team creating global scenario plans. She now speaks about the intelligence of the heart.

This most recent book, *How To Be Loving . . . when your heart is breaking open and the world is waking up*, is also an audiobook + e-book, with a companion journal and deck. Danielle is also the author of *The Fire Starter Sessions*, *White Hot Truth*, and *The Desire Map*, and producer of dozens of meditation kits and online programs for spiritual support.

Her podcast, *With Love, Danielle*, often ranks in iTunes' top 10 for wellness. Most of her offerings—from the Heart Centered membership to classes—are on a pay-what-you-choose basis. Named one of the Top 100 Websites for Women by *Forbes*, millions of people a month visit **DanielleLaPorte.com**.

Her charities of choice are the Ally Global Foundation, helping survivors of human trafficking to rebuild their lives (@allyglobal), TreesSisters reforestation projects (@treesisters_official), and VDay, a movement to end violence against women and girls (vday.org).

She lives in Vancouver, BC. You can find her on most social media platforms **@daniellelaporte**.

#daniellelaporte #howtobeloving #heartcentered

ABOUT CHERYL SORG

The cover art for the *How to Be Loving* book, deck, and journal is by Cheryl Sorg, an artist based in Encinitas, California. Cheryl graduated with honors from the Massachusetts College of Art in Boston. You can find her on Instagram **@cherylsorg**.

ABOUT SOUNDS TRUE

Sounds True is a multimedia publisher whose mission is to inspire and support personal transformation and spiritual awakening. Founded in 1985 and located in Boulder, Colorado, we work with many of the leading spiritual teachers, thinkers, healers, and visionary artists of our time. We strive with every title to preserve the essential "living wisdom" of the author or artist. It is our goal to create products that not only provide information to a reader or listener but also embody the quality of a wisdom transmission.

For those seeking genuine transformation, Sounds True is your trusted partner. At SoundsTrue.com you will find a wealth of free resources to support your journey, including exclusive weekly audio interviews, free downloads, interactive learning tools, and other special savings on all our titles.

To learn more, please visit SoundsTrue.com/freegifts or call us toll-free at 800.333.9185.

HEART CENTERED MEMBERSHIP

Reflection practices and conversations for healing and leading with the intelligence of Love.

Accept yourself on a deeper level. Be more patient with others. Become more loving, more steady, more graceful. Transmute pain into creative power. It's all very possible with steady practice, commitment, connection, and gentleness.

YOU'RE READY: **daniellelaporte.com/membership**

BECOME A HEART CENTERED LEADER + FACILITATOR

Teaching tools for resilience + reflective living to empower the people you serve

For coaches, counselors, corporations, team builders, teachers, wellness professionals, facilitators of change, and idealists of all kinds . . .

30+ exercises, workshops, and conversation formats to use in the workplace, with your clients, students, and communities.

SAVE $111 with code LOVINGFRIENDS on any full-pay option, **daniellelaporte.com/lead**

THE *HOW TO BE LOVING* COLLECTION

Hardcover

E-book

Audiobook

Journal

Deck

MEDITATIONS + PRACTICES + RITUALS

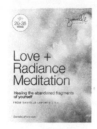

Love +
Radiance
Meditation

Healing the abandoned fragments
of yourself

The Creation
Space
Meditation

Nourish your nervous system,
bring in the generous energy of creativity,
bask in the energy of The Divine.

The Earth
Adoration
Meditation

Sending healing to Mother Earth and
opening our energy channels.

Ocean +
Rose
Meditation

Transmitting waves of zero worries

ALSO BY DANIELLE...
BOOKS. PRINT. DIGITAL. AUDIO.

GIFT A
25% OFF
CODE:

LOVINGFRIENDS
daniellelaporte.com/**shop**
(excludes online courses, membership,
jewelry, and leadership program)

SHARE THE LOVE

If *How to Be Loving* has moved you, please help us spread the principles of Loving Kindness . . .

1. **Send me an email or video testimonial.** Include a link to your site or IG handle, and we can reshare: danielle@daniellelaporte.com

2. **Share it on Instagram.** Post quotes from the book or photos with you and *How to Be Loving* in the world, tagging @daniellelaporte #howtobeloving

3. **Leave a book review at any online bookseller.** It really helps us share the content.

4. If you have **your own social media platform**, create content around how these teachings and practices are shifting your life.

5. **Form a book club, a conversation salon, or healing group** to explore the *How to Be Loving* principles. Focus on a chapter, get together to do one practice, meet to talk about Compassion . . . this is how we heal ourselves and the world.

6. **Become a Heart Centered Leader.** We have licensed coaches + facilitators teaching this content all over the world: daniellelaporte.com/lead

7. Give the Love or get more Love. *How to Be Loving* is available in hardcover, as an e-book, and a 5-hour beautiful audio experience. The audiobook includes enriched practices and inside stories from Danielle.